"Unmasking the Lor[...]
Frank Wilson demo[...]
each other reflect the depth of our relationship with
Christ. In a world where it is too easy to live in isolation,
this book will challenge you to recognize the importance
of accountability."

Josh McDowell, author and speaker

"Frank Wilson takes the first step toward 'unmasking' by
taking off his own mask. With his life as the primary
example, he encourages us to reach out to others, open
our lives to friendship, and trust God to take us beyond
ourselves."

Preston Gillham, President
Lifetime Guarantee Ministries

"This book hits upon a great need in America: how men
can develop personal relationships and accountability
groups. Often the friends and family of a fellow soldier
shot in battle are the last ones to know he has been
wounded. The only cure is a group of men who are
serious about meeting and committed to keeping one
another accountable. For practical, task-focused, bottom-
line guys, *Unmasking the Lone Ranger* is a must."

Phil Downer, President
Christian Business Men's Committee

UNMASKING the LONE RANGER

FRANK WILSON

HARVEST HOUSE PUBLISHERS
Eugene, Oregon 97402

Cover by Koechel Peterson & Associates, Minneapolis, Minnesota

UNMASKING THE LONE RANGER
Copyright © 1998 by Frank Wilson
Published by Harvest House Publishers
Eugene, Oregon 97402

Library of Congress Cataloging-in-Publication Data
Wilson, Frank, 1940–
    Unmasking the lone ranger / Frank Wilson.
      p. cm.
    ISBN 1-56507-852-7 (trade paper)
    1. Christian men—Religious life.   2. Interpersonal relations—Religious aspects—
    Christianity. I. Title.
    BV4528.2.W5 1998
    248.8'42—dc21   98-25105
                                                              CIP

99 00 01 02 03 /BP/ 10 9 8 7 6 5 4 3 2 1

This book is dedicated to those men whose pursuit of kingdom-centered relationships inspired my own quest for a deeper understanding of accountability, friendship, and trust. Through their consistency and compassionate examples they made the task of learning how to love easy. As was done at their home-going celebration, I salute once again, Richard Halverson, John Staggers, Tom Skinner, and Dr. Sam Hines.

Acknowledgments

First, I want to thank my best friend and wife, Bunny, for her crusade in encouraging me to get this book written; for her enormous contribution in proofreading and critiquing the manuscript over and over again. Bob Hawkins Jr., LaRae Weikert, and Carolyn McCready for their enthusiastic reception of the idea and constant reminders of their support for this project. Gene Browning, Joseph Garlington, Henry Greenidge, Chuck Singleton, Carl Martin, James Wilson, Charles Walker, Charles Patrick, Tony Evans, Kenneth Ulmer, Terri McFaddin, Barbara Williams-Skinner, Amelia Parker, Steveland Morris, Smokey Robinson, Larry Carroll, Paul Jackson Jr., Ray Parker Jr., Robb Thompson, Philip Bailey, Lisa Hoggs, Clay Drayton, Don Payne, Mario DuCre, Tom and Denise Mitchell, Ivory Stone, Fred Gladney, Julius West, Peggy Matthews, Debbie DuCre, Gwen Brown, Robert Gordy, Ann Jamerson, Frances Gladney, Scherrie Payne, Sharon Dunn, Nate Fields, Shirley Browning, Estelle Tyne, Ollie Brown, Michelle McKinney-Hammond, Earl Cole, Phillip Myles, Ron O'Guinn, Leonard and Carolyn Caston, Cliff and Audrey Ashe, Michael Spottsville, and many others too numerous to mention, whose steadfast presence in my life have been of inestimable value in learning the meaning of becoming vulnerable and walking together.

Dwight, Michael, Bennett, J.P., Terri, Jason, and Lisa for their valuable feedback during the creative phase of the manuscript.

My children, whose growing closeness to each other, loyalties to their friends, and love for their families underscores what I myself have been learning and attempting to model before them.

My parents, who laid the foundation for my life.

Dr. E.V. Hill, my pastor and mentor, whose life is an inspiration to Bunny and myself, and is, by his example, a picture of friend.

To Chip MacGregor, a friend whose creative genius rose to the occasion while writing under pressure and editing this book.

Bob Hawkins Sr., the flame at Harvest House, whose passion refuses to wane, inspiring us all with his talent and love.

To Teresa, Betty, and Julie, who keep us on the move, and to the tremendous staff and family at Harvest House.

Contents

The Lone Ranger

As a young boy growing up in a sprawling, crime-infested, and segregated urban city, seeing a hero as the underdog was important to me. One of my favorite television shows was "The Lone Ranger," a character created by writer Fran Striker. I have vivid memories of sitting in front of a small black-and-white TV, watching the suspenseful, spine-tingling stories. One of the earliest episodes told the chilling account of when this single law enforcement officer began his crusade.

He had originally been part of a large regiment of Texas Rangers who were savagely ambushed by a ruthless gang of outlaws. Only one man survived the brutal attack; he was badly wounded and left by the side of the road to die. But a lone Indian, sent out on a scouting expedition, stumbled upon the wounded Ranger. He placed the stranger, almost dead, upon his own horse and carried him to a site nearby. In a dense forest that offered seclusion and safety, that Indian built a small camp fire, washed and bandaged the Ranger's wounds, and helped nurse the bullet-riddled man back to health.

As he gradually regained his strength, the Ranger told his benevolent friend, Tonto, his story. He also confided his determination to spend his remaining days defending the unfortunate victims of terror. He dedicated himself to coming to the aid of the distressed and seeking just punishment for criminals.

Following his recovery, the Lone Ranger hid behind a sleekly tailored dark mask in order to conceal his true identity, then proceeded to methodically carry out his vendetta against injustice. He turned up everywhere, rescuing the perishing, the outnumbered, and the outgunned. At the close of each adventure, the Lone Ranger would ride away sitting atop his dependable white stallion, his trusted Indian companion Tonto alongside. As the horse took off in a majestic gallop, a curious bystander or the recipient of his heroic escapades would look around and ask the obvious question: "Who was that masked man?"

"Why, don't you know?" would come the reply, followed by a dramatic pause. "That was . . . *the Lone Ranger!*" The exciting music of the William Tell Overture would rise steadily to its final crescendo as we would hear the Lone Ranger call out in a thunderous voice, "Hi ho, Silver, awaaay!" Off they would go—the Lone Ranger and Tonto, quiet and strong defenders of all that was right, riding into the sunset.

The Second Act

Growing up, I wanted to be like the Lone Ranger. He was the perfect image of what a man should be: strong, silent, hidden, ready to whip the bad guys with his fists. He didn't allow anyone to get close to him, or to discover who he really was behind the mask. The Lone Ranger was too tough for that sort of thing. He enjoyed the protection that mask gave him. While I relished having everyone respect me, I didn't want anyone peeking behind the mask to see the real me.

So I became the Lone Ranger, though in a different sort of way. I could be standing in a room crowded with people and somehow still be all alone. I enjoyed being by myself. I liked having people see the good and strong part of me, without fearing they would get behind the mask and stumble upon something not so good and not nearly as strong. I was comfortable with me, for I was no threat to myself.

The fact is, I functioned well behind the mask. I lived in a safe house, away from the threatening glares of my enemies. I connected with other people enough to get my work done, without letting them find out anything about the real me. And I wasn't alone—many men are referred to as the "strong, silent type." But experience has shown me that most are simply crouched behind a masquerade of silence in order to hide their feelings.

There was a time I would vehemently defend myself if I suspected I was under personal attack. Since I grew up as the underdog in my neighborhood, I had to learn to shield myself. One of my favorite tricks was one I picked up from my dad: In order to protect himself, disarm an opponent, or put my mom in check, he would talk loud and act gruff. It worked for him, so I followed his lead. It usually worked with people in the neighborhood or in business.

Later, after getting married, I used it successfully on my wife, until she started to punish me as a way to get back at me for being gruff, and I in turn would develop a plan to exact revenge. It always proved to be disruptive in our relationship, but somehow it seemed appropriate for the Lone Ranger. If somebody hurts you, find a way to hurt him in return. Regrettably, life is full of ambushes of one kind or another, and retribution can cut both ways;

therefore, as in the movie, the lessons I learned as a kid caused me to set boundaries when it came to people— even the ones claiming to be my friends.

For example, one lazy Saturday morning when I was about ten years old, a street-smart buddy asked Mother if my brother James and I could go into town with him. He said he wanted to show us around, and my mother, somewhat reluctantly, agreed. Upon arriving downtown, we immediately went into a large department store and began checking it out. I was fascinated with the mounds of new merchandise since I usually didn't see many new things except at Christmastime. But while I was running from one toy to the next, having loads of fun, my friend was busy shoplifting. After he ran out of room in his clothing, he hurriedly began stuffing toys and garments beneath our sweaters, saying, "Hold these for me." I may have been a dumb kid, but I wasn't brain-dead. As soon as my friend turned away, I placed all that stuff back onto the shelves. When we exited the store, we were arrested. Fortunately for me, I didn't have any stolen items on my person, so I wasn't charged. But my friend did—and after that day he had a record for shoplifting. The lesson I learned was clear: *Don't trust anyone.* Not even a friend.

As I grew into my teens, my education concerning people continued to advance. One time I told my best friend, Nash, I wasn't sure I had really won my girlfriend Lisa's heart. Sure enough, at a party that night I found Nash in a corner room of my house trying to undermine my credibility and score points with Lisa. He used my honesty against me, and the lesson to not trust anyone was reinforced in my life. Unfortunately, I didn't have a sidekick named Tonto—a silent friend with whom I could share myself. I had to become my own hero, strong and cautious and never allowing anyone too much insight into my life. If you had met me a few years ago, you would have found me to be a little paranoid about people. In my view, I came that way honestly—I started wearing a mask because I needed the protection it offered.

The Mask Lives

I'm not the only one. Long after the television show was canceled and the Lone Ranger's role put in mothballs, the mask lives on. Far too often men will gather for a meeting somewhere and, after an hour of conversation, if one of them were to leave the room, others could still turn and ask, "Who was that masked man?"

We have all learned well the art of surface relationships and shallow conversations. Like the Lone Ranger, we wear masks for the mystique, the protection, and the assurance of privacy. The Lone Ranger was the only one in the regiment to survive the massacre, and he could identify the assailants, so his life was under a constant cloud of danger. His disguise enabled him to sleep comfortably at night without worrying about being discovered. Similarly, we hope our masks offer us some sort of protection while allowing us to project the image of someone's hero.

Think about it: Do you wear a mask? Are you ever worried about being discovered? Is there anyone who really knows the man behind the mask? Come on now, don't try to tell me you never hide behind the cover of a veil in order to conceal your true identity. Our world is full of pretenders. Sometimes we can even be masked strangers to the people in our own homes.

But let me offer one word of advice: If you are content to remain a Lone Ranger, you will miss out on the best parts of life, because no one will ever really know the real you. To be known is to be loved. Are you willing to be completely known by someone . . . or are you too afraid of the risk? How can anyone truly love you when they don't know who you are?

Every day I meet men who desire to change. They're sick and tired of hiding out; they want to take off their masks and let someone discover their true identities. And each time I talk with a man like that, I'm reminded of the road I had to travel and the men who helped me along the way. Somehow the grace of God found me, and the Spirit changed my attitude. I am free from the chains of my past. Except on occasions when I forget I don't have to, I no longer wear a mask.

1
Born to Be a Lone Ranger

Lone Rangers don't just pop up out of nowhere. They are groomed. It takes time to develop a Lone Ranger. In the beginning, they are strangers to everyone—including the one who gave them life. As they grow older, some remain strangers even to those in their own homes. But there is a process that can lead a man from "stranger" to "sidekick," from foreigner to friend, from outsider to insider. It is a process nurtured by love, fostered by friendship, full of joy and pain. It is that process I want to share with you through this book.

I was a very private person. I liked being alone, always have. I loved people, but on my own terms. You could enter my life when it was convenient, congenial, and safe. I was never in the habit of encouraging others to try and know more about me—I even fudged when it came to providing the integral information requested by the physician on a medical history questionnaire or the creditor on a loan application.

I suppose I got that trait from Mother. My mom is also a private person. To this day she is unwilling to discuss how old she is and gets upset when the subject of age comes up, fearing the discussion will eventually get around to discussing her own! She's been like that as long as I can remember. Some would say this is mere vanity, but it is not unusual for people to withhold information about themselves if they feel it might be used against them someday.

You may ask, "How could such information be used against you?" From the perspective of many people I know, it could happen any number of ways. In an environment where youthfulness is considered of greater value than age, and where a physical disability is seen as a liability, a mistake in one's judgment today can lead to a denial of opportunity tomorrow. Some people will attempt to penalize you because they think you are not bright enough, right enough, or light enough. In many cases, just being different can be reason enough to be deemed unworthy.

A Matter of Privacy

The above occurrences do not provide a comprehensive explanation regarding my mother's supersensitivity about age; nevertheless, I think her desire to escape observation is not as much a personal idiosyncrasy as it is a fundamental human characteristic. Sometimes we're afraid that once people really know us, they won't like us. Other times we simply conclude the information is "none of your business."

The early settlers thought privacy so essential during the formation of this nation, they stitched it within the very fabric of the founding document. Anchored by their concept of freedom, privacy was sought to be immortalized in the fourth amendment, today popularly referred to as the "right to privacy act." Simply stated, we cherish our privacy. We don't want to give it up to others. Therefore, it is for a much greater gain that I make the suggestion we plow the fields of suspicion and uncover the soil where seeds of distrust are planted.

As much as we cherish our God-given right to slip out of sight and hide in the shadows, it is good to remember that it is the prince of darkness who dwells there. Behind the wall of seclusion is the place where the enemy spends a great deal of his time, going "to and fro throughout the earth, seeking whom he may devour." Satan prefers to attack the single prey—the ones who have strayed from the flock and are alone and unaccountable. Certainly it is good for me to get away by myself where I can concentrate and seek God's wisdom for decisions, but I must not become too comfortable in isolation. The Scripture says, "A man who isolates himself seeks his own desire; he rages against all wise judgment" (Proverbs 18:1). Consequently, *it is important for me to have a friend with whom I can confidently share some of my private thoughts,* especially those that might someday become a matter of public record or call into question my personal conduct.

Learning to Be Family

You see, I started life in the school of survival. It was a world that appeared harmless, but was deceptive and dangerous. Looking back on those days of growing up, I remember my oldest brother hiding his clothes from me while warning me to stay out of his stuff. James, the second-oldest brother, gave new meaning to the expression "sharp disagreements"—we almost killed each other one time fighting with kitchen knives. My dad was a wonderful man, but even though we lived in the same house, I never knew much about him. I only recently learned that immediately following his teenage years, he departed his hometown in Oklahoma, leaving behind his close relatives while fleeing from the local authorities. It seems that as a young man, my father was sort of a local hero.

Deploring the abject poverty of the poor in his surroundings, he would hitch a ride over to the next county, locate the boxcar on the train where food and clothing were stored, and as the locomotive passed through the neighborhoods he would fling open the door and distribute the merchandise to the people in the community. After months of investigation, the long arm of Oklahoma law reached out for him. Escaping to Texas, my father changed his name and cut off most of his personal ties, including those to his siblings.

A few years later he met and married my mother. Soon after, they began to have children. And though we lived together all of those years, I cannot say with any certainty I ever really knew my father. Family outings? There were none, unless working in the yard on Saturday mornings counts. My father was busy day and night, trying to make ends meet. He didn't open himself up to us, or share his pain or struggle. He was a strong man, whose life was defined by hard work.

My mother, on the other hand, tried to nurture her five children. She never asked us if we wanted to go to church—we went, every Sunday morning and every Sunday night, because she said it was what we must do. Church was the first place I learned the risk involved in assuming people are trustworthy. I was told to "trust and obey" the words of my elders. But when I became a young adult, I saw things in church that caused me to doubt its value. The number of deacons flirting with (and sometimes seducing) other men's wives was appalling. Rumors flew all the time—delicious delicacies, cooked up by those who hungered to see the downfall of anyone who appeared to be genuinely wholesome. It occurred to me that if you cannot rely upon the integrity of church folk, who can you trust?

Occasionally some of our close neighbors would invite me to accompany them on a family trip. They usually gossiped all the way there and all the way home; backstabbing the neighbors, the church members, and the preacher, all the while airing the dirty laundry of their own relatives. One time my uncle and aunt got into a fight. Before I knew what was happening, he had picked up his wife and thrown her to the other side of the room. So when people in the church began talking about the congregation as a "family," I wasn't impressed. I didn't have much of a model upon which to base my understanding. What I knew was that you cannot choose your relatives, and friends can desert you. I was acquainted with the classic concept of family, but I was not well-versed in the knowledge of the Creator's intent. As I reflect on that now, I realize my family and childhood acquaintances shaped me in a very direct way: A bad experience with someone in the past will nearly always affect your attitude about people in the present—and will begin to erode your trust in God.

Self-Examination

I came to the conclusion a few years ago that if I really had brothers and sisters in the family of God, I was going to have to learn how to have healthy relationships with my siblings. What led me onto this path? A self-examination. In looking at my life, I realized that in many ways I was a stranger in my own house. I was intimate with no one. There wasn't a single person who knew my heart. I felt challenged by the complexities of life. Then the living example of a couple of brothers and some clear instructions from the Bible caused me to examine my situation.

How can we as believers learn the art of interpersonal relationships and get a grip on things like parenting and mentoring, unless we open up and discuss our individual ideas with someone else? Do we test our personal beliefs out on our own families and friends first, even if that means making mistakes and messing up their lives, or do we agree that we need help in learning how to be the best dad, husband, or companion that a man can become? Shouldn't we also inspect our lives through the observation of a friend? I've watched too many men foul up their families, discard them, exonerate themselves from responsibility, then write a book about their experiences afterward. Can we not see better the span of our lives through the added dimension of an extra set of eyes?

God desires to use each one of us to help other members of the family mature. We protect each other by being honest with one another. We expand and establish the kingdom of God as we expose our walk with Christ to others. His kingdom is attractive when the righteousness in our lives is evident to those around us. It begins in our families, and spreads to our schools, churches, jobs, and neighborhoods. As we express Christ's righteousness through our individual lifestyles, His name is exalted. But if we are afraid to let anyone know us, or challenge our thinking by seeing what is in our hearts, we restrict our individual capacity for growth within the kingdom of God. The Bible exhorts us to "let brotherly love continue"(Hebrews 13:1), and to do so will mean we have to begin opening up ourselves to others.

Our lives together should indicate that we are committed to one other. The root word for *family* is the same as that for *familiar*—it means to draw close to other people so that they know you. We are to treat those in God's family as brothers and sisters. That suggests our family members are to be intimately acquainted with one another, informal and at ease.

Loving Everybody

The moment I submitted my life to Jesus and became a member of His family, something in my heart changed. When I fell in love with the Savior, I knew I was supposed to love His people as well. But I was still a little suspicious of them. Most believers are quick to say, "I love everybody," but I've discovered that *it is sometimes easier to love a group of people you don't know, than it is to love one person you do.* We like the idea of everyone meeting Christ, connecting with them from a distance and being nice, but we don't want them to get too close. The reigning philosophy governing these relationships is, "If you don't tell me your problems, I promise you I won't tell you mine."

If you think that's too hard of a statement, let me confess something: What was true of the people in the church was also true of me. I loved everybody. I had this spiritually sophisticated, universal kind of love that allowed me to sound great to anyone who asked. But one day God's Word confronting me said, "We know that we have passed from death unto life, because we love the brethren. He who does not love his brother abides in death" (1 John 3:14). And I was abiding in death. I didn't know what real love was. What would genuine love for the brethren look like? For instance, I can remember as a kid hearing ol' Miss Sally say in church, "If you don't have anything good to say about somebody, don't say anything at all." But when she got around her friends, Miss Sally, who didn't like the minister's wife, would proceed to talk about that woman as though she was the worst thing to happen to the church.

If Miss Sally overheard me saying something bad about someone, she was quick to remind me that was wrong. But if I challenged her with, "I heard you and your friends talking about the pastor's wife the other day," she could excuse herself with, "Young man, don't do as I do, just do as I say." I learned to accept that philosophy in a world where everyone does what is right in his own eyes. But in the community of faith, where we are to represent "light" and "salt" in the world, saying and doing ought to be synonymous (1 John 3:16). Not seeing a picture in person of the kind of unconditional love that ought to exist between brothers, I glossed over it and put it behind me.

Therefore, when I met Christ, there remained something missing in my life: a genuine, unconditional love for others. When I met Bunny, I was certain I had found the missing piece. She was an answer to prayer. God's gift to me. I married the one person I desired to show all of my love—but unfortunately, I had never learned how to love. It was too much of a risk. If there was an individual anywhere in the world I wanted to know me, it was Bunny. Yet I didn't know how to show her who I was. It was easier for me to give her a gift than it was to give her myself. As a result, in the beginning of our marriage, Bunny deserved far more of me than the little she got. It was much safer for me to abort trust, put on a front, and keep my real self hidden. And so, like most of the men I knew, I hid.

That is, until the meeting.

2
Setting Up the Drama

Brenda, a wonderful teacher and zealous fellow member in our local church assembly, noticed that I was bringing some of the musicians and entertainers I worked with to the worship service trying to disciple them. A life-changing encounter with Christ had greatly increased my interest in serving Him, and it seemed like common sense to start sharing my new faith with friends, family, and coworkers in the entertainment industry. Brenda told me about a friend of hers, a Christian leader from the community, and excitedly informed me he would be getting in touch. A few days later the friend, interested in expanding the reach of his ministry, telephoned the recording studio where I was working and arranged for us to speak in person. At our initial meeting we prayed and discussed the organizing of a weekly home-based Bible study and fellowship time, targeting the creative and business personalities within the entertainment industry. Several weeks went by with much prayer, discussion, and the agreement of many, before we launched the group. The teacher, an easy-to-know kind of brother, was also a very focused individual with a keen mind. Soft-spoken, with a compassionate and nonaggressive teaching style, he effectively introduced many of those in atten-dance to the one true God each week, persuading numerous souls to accept Jesus as their Savior.

The Principal Players

Approximately ten months passed, when one evening following our Bible Study, we heard the doorbell ring. In walked Gene Browning. The first thing you notice about Gene is his laugh—it bubbles up from an underground well of personal joy, constantly flowing from a living spring and fed by a time of regular worship. He is tall, with a broad physique, sparkling brown eyes, and richly endowed with a chocolate-golden tone to his skin. He had come to Los Angeles from our nation's capital to see our teacher. Due to what they called a "covenant relationship" between them, they had pledged to always view each other as family, to demonstrate concern and commitment through their constant encouragement, confrontation, and mutual accountability.

After agreeing the two would get together the next morning, Gene hunkered down for the rest of the evening and relaxed. Perhaps as a way of breaking the ice, he began to tell me about his wife and children. Up until that point in my life, I don't believe I had ever met anyone so refreshingly honest and transparent. Gene began to talk about his personal struggles as a father, his failures as a husband, and some present difficulties in his growth as a man. The conversation was fascinating to me, because here was a man singing my song! I had thought it was my original composition until I met Gene Browning. That night, he disclosed the steps he was taking to alleviate some of the pressures he was facing in his life. For example, he was anxious about the negative influences of the culture on his children, so he had begun to take them out on individual dates. He wanted to strengthen the foundation of their self esteem while bringing clarity and openness to their relationship.

"Frank," he roared, while tossing in a few bellows of sheer delight, "I'm really getting to know my kids for the first time. It's great!" Then his whole body seemed to laugh. I was thinking to myself, "Wow, I've only known this guy for 30 minutes and I've already learned a couple of things from him I can use." It is amazing how much you can glean from others if you slow your mind down long enough to listen to somebody else talk.

We went on for another hour or so until everyone started to stretch and yawn and rise to leave. The next day Gene left town, but even after his return to Washington, he and I chatted often. Usually he would have some other person on the phone with him, or a few minutes into our conversation he would get another friend of his on the three-way line by saying, "You just have to meet him, Frank. Hold on." It was through this connection I made another new friend: John Staggers.

"How are you doing, mate?" was John's initial greeting to me. "Gene tells me you're out there in LA walking with Harold." I had no idea what he was talking about, but it was clear to me I should have, so I pretended to go along with the conversation, deciding to figure out the details later. "I'm glad you made friends with Gene," he said to me. "He really gets to know people in a hurry, doesn't he? Do you want to know his secret? Being with Gene is like coming into contact with a can opener—he will gradually pry off your top, pour you out on a table, and look at the contents of your life."

I told him that I agreed with his assessment—Gene had immediately made me feel that we were close friends.

"It works," John told me, "as long as you are not masquerading as the Lone Ranger, concealing your true identity. It's uncomfortable for the average man who has spent a lifetime constructing a disguise. You see, Frank, we're all imperfect, but we like folks to think we're not. We try to hide our flaws, though they are the very areas God needs to get at in order to change us. That is one of the greatest reasons why we need one another." Then he paused and added, "We need to help each other get rid of our masks. It is essential to our growth. I don't know why it is, but some of us even try to hide who we are from God. When all the while, He just wants to take us higher in Him."

At that moment, I felt my life was never going to be the same. I was beginning to talk with a new type of Christian—ones who were willing to share themselves openly with others. I had never known anyone like that, and I could already feel myself being drawn into a relationship with these men.

Keeping My Appointment

Not long after that, I found myself on a 727 heading for the capital. Having just finished an appointment in Atlanta, I was 35,000 feet in the air when we suddenly were in the middle of a thunderstorm, bouncing through dark, ominous clouds. Since I had neither family, close friends, nor business interests in Washington, DC, I began wondering what had compelled me to commit my time and expense to get there in the midst of a storm. But, in plain terms, I *had* to go. I felt commissioned by God. I was responding to the request of five young men doing hard time at a maximum security prison located outside of the city. I didn't know them, but I was seeking the center of God's will for my life. I was learning to be open, to go wherever His Spirit might lead me.

An article in *Jet* magazine, which carried a picture of me at a Bible study in Pasadena with several Hollywood entertainers, caught the prisoners' attention. They casually mentioned the same to John Staggers during one of his visits with them, and wondered aloud the possibility of my coming to see them. John asked, "What did you say his name was again?"

"Frank Wilson," they told him.

"I've met him," John surprised them, adding, "I'll see if I can get in touch with him."

A few weeks later I was participating in an evangelistic event with Dr. E.V. Hill at Moorehouse College in Atlanta. Several of us traveled from California, but instead of going back to Los Angeles with everyone else, I rerouted my return trip through Washington. "The next time you come to the East Coast," John had said to me, "there are some brothers in prison who are asking if you would be willing to come and visit them." The idea was intriguing to me. I had never given thought to the fact that since God is our Father, all of His children are our brothers and sisters. I assumed these men weren't there for the same reasons that had landed Paul and Silas or Peter and John in jail. Yet because of the circumstances and channel through which their request had traveled, I believed it to be the will of God that I make the effort to visit.

I arrived in Washington, DC, early that evening. After spending the night in the city, John and I departed for the prison facility, located in Virginia. Once we cleared security, we were escorted by the warden into a large but sparsely furnished hall where we were joined by five inmates. They ranged in age from early twenties to late thirties. Each of them was very articulate, warm, and humble. I was told their offenses ranged from simple assault to robbery and murder.

But none of this is what stood out in my mind. What intrigued me the most was their commitment to one another. Contrary to my initial conclusion, they were not bonded to each other for the sake of mental, emotional, or physical survival. With John as their teacher, they had welded their lives together for the purpose of making a positive difference, advancing God's kingdom inside that place now called their "home." These guys had become "brothers" in a way that was completely foreign to me.

Long after the day had ended, I sat alone at the table beside my bed, looking into God's Word. That meeting galvanized my thoughts, narrowed my focus, and caused me to rethink my activities. Although in prison, these guys saw themselves as *brothers*. I had a desire to explore this type of kingdom-centered relationship. In some way, I recognized that even though they were in prison, they had something I didn't have.

Cause for Alarm

Back in the city the following morning, John and Gene took me to what they described as a "weekly prayer meeting." Following a period of prayer and fellowship filled with laughter, praise reports, and favorite hymns, John and a local pastor took the time to get to know me better. I was doing the same old thing, observing them and keeping my thoughts to myself, but I noticed that the fellowship among these brothers flowed well together. It was uncanny how intimately they seemed to know one another, completely uncharacteristic of my own experiences. After a few exchanges of common theological truths, John let loose with the first of several insightful comments, obliterating my nice, neat spiritual comfort zones.

For five minutes I had been going on about how I was contributing monthly to try and help out a mutual friend who just couldn't seem to get his head above water financially. I was feeling proud and significant, waiting for a pat on the back for my ongoing commitment to this brother which paralleled strongly, I thought, their dedication to one other. No one, however, said anything until

John interrupted my exercise of self-congratulation with, "Frank, why are you being so disobedient to God?"

"What?" I didn't know what he was talking about. "What do you mean?"

He continued by saying, "Frank, can't you see that God has put holes in the brother's bucket? It doesn't matter how much you help, he is not going to be able to hold onto any of it. All you are doing is delaying the inevitable and getting in God's way of teaching him a very valuable lesson in stewardship and self-control." Before that had sunk all the way in, he zinged me with a second, more stunning pronouncement: "Frank, you can't go any deeper in Christ than you are willing to go with another brother."

Well, that did it. First, he tells me I don't have the right to give to whomever I want, then he tells me my relationship with someone else determines the depth of my walk in Christ. *That's nothing but spiritual elitism*, I thought to myself. Yet I had to admit, his words shook me. I couldn't wait to get back home to my familiar surroundings. At first I didn't think I needed to pray about any of this. But while I was on the plane jetting back to Los Angeles, I rehearsed several aspects of the trip in my head. And though I tried to forget, I couldn't deny the imprint upon my mind of that meeting, nor could I shake the impact of John's words. They clung to me, haunting my mind. That's when I decided to talk to God about it.

Meeting the Challenge

Through several weeks of prayer, meditation, and Bible study, I thought about the words of John Staggers: *You can't go any deeper in Christ than you are willing to go with another brother.* If you have ever met a man whose entire life was dedicated to serving "the least of these my brothers," it was John. He was socially, spiritually, and intellectually solid as a rock. I wrestled with the meaning of what he had said, and wondered what it would look like in a practical sense to "go deep" with a brother.

One morning God spoke to me from His Word: "As I have loved you...you also love one another" (John 13:34). Apparently, God was calling me to practice *loving* people. "For he who does not love his brother whom he has seen, how can he love God whom he has not seen? And this commandment we have from Him: that he who loves God must love his brother also" (1 John 4:20,21).

I knew that I loved God, but how could I verify it so that I was not just loving "in word or tongue only, but in deed"? Some people will insist that by working hard for God, you prove your love. But some of us work hard because we are workaholics by nature. Others love God in order to be recognized, or to climb higher up the ladder of success in the field of ministry. Many involve themselves in one program after another, tackle one social issue after another, and belong to every auxiliary in the church just to keep busy. But God knows us and loves each of us, *one person at a time*. He knows the very number of hairs on our heads. It is not just that God knows us; He's *concerned* about us.

Jesus suggests in His Word that an expression of my love for Him is best evidenced through benevolent actions toward another brother. When I realized that, I began to think about all the things I was consistently trying to do to help others. Then the Spirit reminded me that these philanthropic activities in the world are often not done out of love. They're done for me to make me feel good, or for a pat on the back, perhaps out of sympathy, but not for love. With that thought, I realized it was time I developed some real relationships with other Christian men.

3
The Meeting

The first time I visited New Zealand, we stayed at a hotel directly across the roadway from a four-star seafood restaurant. After several meals there, I discovered all of the entrées on the menu were excellent. The desserts, however, which I seldom eat after a meal, were stupendous—highlighted by a soft, fluffy meringue dish known simply as *pavlova*. As soon as you ate it, the substance would instantly dissolve in your mouth, leaving only the memory of its rich and wonderful flavor. Upon returning to the United States, I searched diligently for a place that served pavlova, visiting many different restaurants in various cities. I was unable to locate a single serving. So each time we return to New Zealand, I find an establishment that serves it and make a regular date for dining.

In a similar way, there is nothing more delightful than knowing you have been with God and have experienced His sweet presence. Then, when you stray from His will, every remembrance of His fellowship unleashes a longing within you to go back to that place and tarry. If you have ever enjoyed the privilege of being introduced to the Person of Jesus, you know your introduction was only the first stage of a lasting new existence. When you meet Christ as Savior, you enter a world that offers a whole range of opportunities, each one yearning to be explored. "Taste and see that the Lord is good," says the psalmist. "Blessed is the man who puts his trust in Him." A single sample of the glory of God will cause any heart to ache for another taste.

The Lord's goodness was evident to me. When I met Him, my life changed forever. Now He was leading me to experience something new: honest loving relationships with others. Having tasted it just a bit through my friends in Washington, I was ready for a local encounter.

A Love Like This

Think of how God has loved you. Every day He is pulling for you to win. Even when He knew you were going to blow it, disregard His advice, and get yourself into deep trouble, He still placed upon the back burner of His agenda whatever He was doing and came to your rescue. An old church hymn intoned this rhetorical question about Jesus: "Would He devote that sacred head for such a worm as I?"

That is the head that was torn by the thorns pressed down upon His brow as He stumbled beneath the weight of the cruel cross He bore to Calvary. The Lord Jesus demonstrated for us the depth of His love when He died for us poor sinners on the cross. Just before embarking on that journey, He told His followers, "All men will know that you are My disciples, if you love one another."

As I reflected on the people I had met and the truths I had begun to discover in Scripture, I came to a decision: "I'm ready, Lord." Then I thought to myself, "But where do I begin?" After a few weeks of pondering and pressing God for more light on the subject, I said to a close friend, "Do you realize we can't go any deeper in Christ than we are willing to go with each other?" I let it sink in a bit before continuing. "We need each other in order to learn how to put into practice God's greatest commandment to 'love Him with all our heart, mind, soul and strength.'" Then I asked him, "How do you think we should be loving God?"

My friend said he wasn't sure what I was getting at, so we began to talk about our relationship as brothers in Christ. True love for other people is motivated by our love for God. Jesus claimed, "If you love Me, [you will] keep My commandments. . . . A new commandment I give to you, that you *love one another*; as I have loved you, that you also love one another" (John 14:15; 13:34). I told my friend that I think those words mean we ought to love each other better. Only when we love God with all of our being is His unconditional love toward others released through us. And not only His love, but His power, peace, and presence.

My friend just looked at me for a minute before replying, "Since we both want that, let's get started."

The Beginning

I called a gathering to explain the meeting I wanted to start. Four men showed up: my close friend Carl, my older brother James, and two mutual friends, Chuck and Charles. The first thing we did was agree that we would meet in order to learn how to love one another with God's love and help each other grow. We all agreed that you learn to truly love people when you spend time with them. The five of us discovered that even though we had been going to church together, been in Bible studies and on fishing trips, we knew very little about one another. We didn't know simple things, like each other's birth dates, or children's names, nor were we familiar with the deeper issues in each other's lives, like the condition of our marriages, our struggles with the flesh, and our fears concerning the future.

Amos 3:3 asks, "Can two walk together, except they are agreed"? And how, I wondered, can they be agreed if they never discuss issues that are common components in each of their lives? How will we know our brothers' struggles and strivings unless we talk about them? And how can we talk unless we get together and spend time?

Most of us were so lax in keeping commitments that we could make an appointment with each other and cancel without even calling to explain. Surprisingly, we didn't think it important enough to humbly apologize for standing up a friend.

Realizing this forced us to keep our plan simple. First, we agreed to meet. Second, we agreed to meet on time. No one's time is more valuable than a friend's. Third, we agreed to meet before most of us had to be at work. We settled on 6:00 A.M., every Thursday morning. We would have no agenda except to show up on time and begin practicing how to love one another unconditionally. All of us soon discovered that just being together, because we desired to be, helped develop a bit of the love we all were seeking. It was a fresh perspective for us all.

Goals of the Group

This would not be a Bible study, with its built-in arena for arguments. Neither was it a prayer meeting in which we would hide our needs behind nice-sounding requests and words. Our meeting was to be a Thursday morning men's fellowship time, where we would learn how to be real, reliable, and transparent. Over time, the ages ranged from teenagers to senior citizens, with different races and different denominations. We met every week, and we refrained from asking anyone else to attend because we wanted to avoid all distractions and focus on three primary goals:

1. We desired to learn *how to love each other,* based upon the undiluted Word of God.

2. We would work at *developing a practical demonstration* of the appropriate response of love and commitment with those closest to us.

3. Finally, we would *wait for the Spirit's prompting* before inviting another friend to the fellowship, assuring us that it would always remain a meeting of brothers and an avenue to God's family.

One thing we've learned is that the prince of darkness prefers to attack single prey—the ones who have strayed from the flock. Therefore we decided we would be stronger if we stuck together. It soon became apparent that each of us sees better when he can look at his life through the eyes of another, so we began listening to the perspectives of others. It was also clear that God planned all along, to use others to help us see Himself more clearly.

Together we made an agreement: We pledged to "always see each other as family." The men in that group decided to weld their lives together—a few good men working for the purpose of making a difference in each other's lives. And since an expression of love for God is best weighed upon a scale of benevolent action, we began seeking ways to minister to those around us.

Taking the Test

The men who were at that first meeting began exploring character issues—a test of sorts, by which we could gauge our love. These were the things we had to ask ourselves if we were to see where we stood.

1. Do you easily insinuate wrongdoing, or do you quickly give your brother the benefit of the doubt?

2. Do you carefully weigh your brother's opinion when it is different from your own before coming to a final conclusion?

3. Would you attempt to diminish another person's worth by making uncomplimentary remarks if you are both trying out for the same position?

4. Do you try and dominate the conversation and manipulate everyone's opinion in order to have things your own way?

5. Do you disclose intimate conversations with others?

6. Do you make up stories about other people that are not true?

You probably know several men who would fail this test, then don their mask, pretending to be a champion of all the people. But there is no hiding from God—either we love our brothers and demonstrate that love, or we are phonies, pretending to love but not doing anything loving.

Take a minute and work through those questions in your own life. If you are honest with yourself, can people see the love of God in your life? How helpful would it be to begin meeting with a group of fellow believers, to try and develop support and accountability?

As you begin thinking about starting your own meeting, so that you too can begin to unmask the Lone Ranger, I would like to suggest a few practical steps. First, *ask God to show you two or three men* you already consider friends and brothers. Invite them to join you in reading the first three chapters of this book and make a decision about pursuing a relationship.

Second, *agree to take your relationship with Christ to a deeper level* through a focused approach of learning together mutual love, commitment, and accountability. Don't let it become a surface social time, and don't try and turn it into a prayer meeting. Insist that the focus of your time together will be on developing your walk with Christ and with your brothers.

Third, *select a convenient weekly time for you all to meet*. (You will want to avoid a time that could easily conflict with anyone's schedule.) Agree to meet consistently for a year, and use this meeting time as an opportunity for getting to know one another more intimately.

Finally, *pray earnestly for one another and for a move of God* upon your hearts. Share Scripture, not for determining its broadest meanings, but in specific reference to gaining insight for personal living. How does a passage in the Bible help you to see Christ clearer in responding to areas in your life? What does it teach you? How should you apply it?

After a while, evaluate your meetings' impact and discuss making the practice of walking together a permanent pursuit. You will soon discover this exercise of walking in a committed relationship will be a great aid in your maturing in Christ.

4
The Man Behind the Mask

William Shakespeare once wrote that all the world is a stage, and all the men and women merely players. No matter where you go today, life is full of actors. From the classroom to the courtroom, the president to the playground, the preacher to the pew, we can see a whole range of promising actors. But does anyone know who these people really are?

Many thought it was interesting when Ronald Reagan became president—an actor playing the role of a politician. Little did we know at the time that many of our politicians were already great actors. In Christ's day, they were called "hypocrites"—people in masks, pretending to be someone else.

But let's not bash politicians. The fact is, actors are everywhere. During the day they are sitting in boardrooms, and at night they are around the dinner table. Too soon we are devastated when we discover it was all an act. Yet it remains the quest of those very same people, the actors, to find "genuineness" in others. "Where are the people without masks?" they wonder. Before exposing themselves, they must first find someone they believe is real. The truth is, before they tip their hand, they want to see yours.

True Fellowship

Since the fall of man in the Garden of Eden, he has sought to find something with which to cover himself. But covering up is not what most of us need right now. Instead, we need exposure, so that the darkness in our lives may be scattered. As believers, we are called to fellowship—time and shared lives with other men. We need to step out of the blackened theaters and into the light of life, where others can see the transforming radiance of Christ.

Darkness is an illusion. We need light. As the apostle John put it, "If we walk in the light as He is in the light, *we have fellowship one with another*" (1 John 1:7). True fellowship with God and each other is what our soul desires. It takes place as we walk in the light of God's Word.

Unfortunately, most men don't experience true fellowship. Instead, they use "limited access" as a substitute, in order to protect themselves and cover up their imperfections. I remember attending a seminar several years ago with Zig Ziglar, the internationally famous motivational speaker. He told a story about a man who was visiting a church one Sunday morning and noticed several people he knew in attendance. Upon seeing them, he commented, "I could never join this church—there are too many hypocrites in it." Zig's reply was simple: "Don't let that stop you, friend. There's always room for one more!" We roared with laughter. However, the fact is, Zig was right. Too many of us are hypocrites—men in masks.

In Luke 6:42 we find the Lord saying these words: "How can you say to your brother, 'Brother, let me remove the speck that is in your eye,' when you yourself do not see the plank that is in your own eye? Hypocrite! [literally, *Actor!*] First remove the plank from your own eye, and then you will see clearly to remove the speck that is in your brother's eye." In other words, before I try to identify the problem that is in *your* life, I first need to get *my own* house in order. By keeping the spotlight on others, a man is attempting to keep it off himself. Pretending to have his life together, he becomes nothing more than an actor playing the part of an expert.

The Challenge to Change

Do you ever ask yourself, "Why do we pretend?" It takes a lot of energy to keep a cover-up going. It also creates a mountain of mental stress, and though it is perceived by many to be a necessary evil for a greater gain, my experience has taught me that most men want to make a change. We desire true fellowship. But for the majority of us, it is easier to talk about than it is to accomplish.

Why should we want to change? Because hiding beneath that tough exterior of yours, behind that mask you wear, is a brother I long to meet. There is an exquisite person inside you that God has designed, but it is concealed by the one you have constructed for your own comfort. I cannot allow my accomplishments in life to camouflage my condition. As my good friend Leonard Caston once said, "The plan may be perfect, but what about the price?" The covering I wear may be beautiful, but does it compare in any way with the potential of the person it keeps under wrap?

A few years ago I heard a song by Michael Jackson entitled "Man in the Mirror." In it he fervently intoned, "I'm looking at the man in the mirror, I'm asking him to change his ways." Recently that song came back to me, and I started to pay attention to the lyrics. I thought about those words in light of all my past mistakes—the pain I have caused, the multiple problems I have created for my family, and the predicaments I've found myself in. As I suggested earlier, I am a product of my upbringing, the environment I grew up in, and the people I chose to spend my early years with. Each of them has either added to or subtracted from my life. But even if I had grown up in ideal surroundings, I would still be far from my peak potential because of my present condition: *I'm a sinner.* The Bible says, "All have sinned and fall short of the glory of God" (Romans 3:23). That includes me and you. As a sinner, I'm bound to fall short of the ideal man.

But you see, God has ordained more for my life than I can possibly imagine. When I ponder the face of the man I see in my mirror, I know I am not the only one asking Him to change my ways. My wife, my children, some of my friends, and especially the Holy Spirit who lives in me are all asking me to make a change. I want to be better. I want to be more like Christ. But I can't become all God wants me to be alone.

The words of the psalmist David challenged me one morning during my devotions: "I thought about my ways [my tendencies, my habits, how I handle certain difficult situations, and the direction in which I was headed], and turned my feet to Your testimonies" (Psalm 119:59). When I looked at my own patterns of operation, I was persuaded to ask the man in the mirror to change his ways. You see, I want to be the epitome of God's design for me. I desire to walk in victory, to achieve my maximum potential, and I don't want my sinful, selfish desires to mess it up.

Looking in the Mirror

Have you ever thought about your ways? What part of your past are you still practicing? When you look at that man in the mirror, do you still see the face of anger and bitterness hidden behind a deceptive smile? We men often have a tendency to keep imperfections hidden, but God says He has taken away all the old ways. That old, sinful man is dead and buried if you know the Lord. "For he hath made him to be sin for us, who knew no sin; that we might be made the righteousness of God in him" (2 Corinthians 5:21 KJV).

As I pondered those words one morning, a thought struck me: Maybe I need to spend more time thinking about who I *am* in Christ, and less time reflecting about who I *was* before meeting Him. When you stop looking at yourself and start looking at Jesus, your perception of yourself changes. You recognize you can have fellowship with other people, because God has changed you. Remember, you will never see your destiny when looking in the wrong direction.

The best thing we can do as brothers in Christ is to remind each other that we are all imperfect, but loved nonetheless. God loves you and me, even though we both sin and fail Him at times. And He loves me through my brothers, for they continue to support me even when they watch me fail.

When I look in the mirror, I don't see a failure. I see a man who is loved by God, and who sees that love poured out regularly through his brothers in the faith. It's that love they share with me that encourages me in my down times. It's that love that frees me to take off my mask and be myself.

Art Imitating Life

One day I decided to make a special meal. I had already put in most of the ingredients when I considered the added dimension of flavoring it with rosemary leaves, which are, on their own, somewhat bitter. Not wishing to lose the consistency of the broth nor the principal thrust of the taste, I ground up the rosemary leaves as finely as I could before adding them to the dish. As it neared completion, the aroma created from the merging of the different flavors made for one new, unique, and sumptuous enticement. It slowly wafted its way outside, perched upon the wings of the warm mid-afternoon autumn air, drawing the attention of some visitors coming up the driveway.

When they entered the house, it caused them to immediately inquire, "What is that?" Of course, the great chefs (a title for which I do *not* qualify) who have studied their craft over a period of time will be the first to tell you that one of the most important keys to fine cooking is the skill to mix sweet, tart, bitter, and bland together for the ultimate flavorful experience. From the intriguing blend of flavors comes something beautiful.

In a similar way, the noted masters of music (Bach, Beethoven, Mozart) astonished their contemporaries with an unparalleled ability to create music. They would combine major and minor keys, mixing and augmenting their sounds perfectly, so the descriptions of their compositions had the distinction of being called divinely inspired. Likewise the great artists whose paintings are today termed masterpieces were able to mingle and mesh the same colors commonly found in existence during all ages. But through their imagination, special artists could capture the grandeur and depths of real life, command a response of genuine compassion, and move one to tears with shadows and shades stroked upon a canvas of parched paper.

Yet to a far greater degree, God, through His awesome creative power, is making for Himself a glorious bride, an eternal masterpiece. He formed us from nothing. He arranged for the circumstances of our lives, and is in the process of bringing us all together into one magnificent marvel as we mature, before creation, in the faith.

Think for a moment what it might be like if He could use you and me together, without our man-made masks, prepackaged prejudices, and self-imposed limitations. We know He specializes in making imperfection perfect for

His purposes. So when sometimes you feel ground down, chopped up, shaken, and whipped, don't fret. Give God space. He is at work, smoothing out your rough edges and mending your brokenness. He has placed men around you as His assistants, instruments of His refining process. Be open.

In order for God to have His way in the shaping of our character, we must be prepared to enter into relationships that make us uncomfortable, and that force us to make adjustments in ourselves. Your mask stands between you and your brothers. Take it off and let them behold the real you change before their very eyes.

5
What Makes a Man?

Not long ago I asked a group of guys during a men's conference, "What are some of the common myths you hear about manhood today?" Their responses were varied and passionate. The first couple of answers I was familiar with: "Real men don't cry; they don't feel hurt or pain." They continued with, "Men are not romantic." Then came, "They are not afraid." However, the one theme that played through all the answers was clear: "Men are not emotional." These myths about manhood are the messages men send because of the masks they wear.

Today, many men are simply puzzled about what makes a man. We may not admit it, but it's true. We don't know the difference between a mature man and an immature one. We are confused, comparing a man's responsibilities to a woman's. We are puzzled about headship in the home. Men believe they are ordained to be the boss, and that the Bible teaches there is only one Person whose authority and power is greater, but they don't know how to put that truth into practice.

In some homes, the wives have no respect for the wishes of their husband. Neither do the children for their father. Do you know why? Because he got fired! God gave the man the authority in that home to be its head, but he confused headship with lordship. The family already has a Lord—what they need is a family head.

At our house, Dad was the boss—period. Yet none of us really knew him. Still, his style of leadership in the home was the only one I knew. So after I got married, I ruled with an iron fist. However, our families are not looking for some ominous and oppressive force to sit down upon them. They need to see a head who leads by example, a leader who is submitted to God's leading. That is my challenge now that I am the head of my own house. *God is not looking for a leader; He is looking for a man He can lead.* Unfortunately, to be led means a man must trust his leader, and most men are afraid to put complete trust in anyone. His family, in turn, is afraid to trust him.

How do we go from trusting the world's system to trusting God's? The strength of trust is security. We must become so secure in God, we would say as Job did in the midst of his greatest trials, "Though He slay me, yet will I trust Him" (Job 13:15). The way to begin that task is to begin being honest with our emotions.

Unmasking His Emotions

Men and women are different in a variety of ways, but there is one area in which we are not nearly as different as people like to believe. In our culture, we have a tendency to think of women as being emotional, and men as being logical. From childhood, men are taught to keep their emotions in check. "Big boys don't cry," we're told. And since we've not been encouraged to show our feelings, the open display of emotions makes many men nervous. But the Bible says that *God gave us our emotions.* In fact, the Lord Jesus Himself is emotional, rejoicing in celebration and crying at the death of a friend. So this suppression of natural, healthy human sentiment contributes to emotional adolescence and immaturity in men, particularly in relationships.

No matter what the culture says, men are emotional beings. Society has taught us to suppress that aspect of our nature, and lacking experiences that would develop our understanding and ensure comfort, our emotions remain vulnerable, immature, and in need of protection.

Think of emotions like the meters on the instrument panel of an airplane. The gauges indicate what is going on underneath the hood and inside the cabin. A gauge that starts blinking red is in trouble. If the area affected is not addressed, an eruption of some sort might very well occur. In much the same way, emotions are an immediate response to external stimuli. They are often a primary reaction to your environment, and may involve certain psychological changes (like your pulse rate or your body temperature). These feelings are mechanisms designed by God as *an internal indicator of an outside occurrence*. In many instances, they are meant to get our attention. A man's tendency to close up and deny other people access to his emotions in order to closely guard his feelings is an attempt to remain in control. We love to be in charge of our emotions, but a "controlled" and unacknowledged emotion can cause big problems.

Consider the danger if one is successful in keeping the meters on the instrument panel of an airplane from displaying an accurate readout of what is going on inside. An explosion or a crash is imminent. Denying the truth doesn't make the problem go away. How much more important is it for men to develop in the area of emotional maturity when human lives and relationships are at stake! Eventually anything growing on the inside of you has to emerge on the outside. A frustrated, angry, or unstable emotional state will soon lead to an unhappy mental condition and an unhealthy physical state. Except for those whose sensitivities are matured, or the ones who use their portrayal of feelings purely for manipulative purposes, men hide much of their emotions inside. It's a wonder their lives last as long as they do!

The Stealth Mode

Instead of learning how to manage our emotions, men are often rewarded for masking or camouflaging them. We learn various techniques for protecting our feelings, most of which are destructive in relationships. One method of protection we use I call the "stealth mode." That is, we just vanish off the radar screen.

Jim is married to Susan. She has made a decision about a very expensive purchase that she is on the verge of finalizing. When she asks him his opinion about it, she makes it clear by how she presents the scenario that her mind is already made up. She is submitting to the principle of family order, but in her mind it's already a done deal. Jim has mixed emotions regarding how to respond. In one regard, he is upset that she is asking him to rubber-stamp a decision she has already made. He does not agree with the purchase and believes it is a bad deal. On the other hand, he does not wish to appear petty, insecure, or controlling. When she brings up the purchase, he doesn't know how to respond. Saying nothing, he feels manipulated, inadequate, and angry. Up goes the shield.

This man's feelings are telling him that something needs addressing, but at the moment his emotions are calling the shots. He becomes silent, short, and withdrawn. Not knowing how to respond emotionally, he employs his "cloaking device," masking his true feelings. When she asks him, "What's wrong, Baby?" His response is a curt, "Nothing." If she persists, he will possibly reiterate with, "I said nothing's the matter. I'm just tired,

OK?" This buildup will eventually end up in an outburst. He'll often hide his vulnerability behind a sharp, blunt exterior and an aggressive, macho attitude. So true is this that the more brusque a man is on the surface, the more emotion he is protecting inside. Consequently, people who think they know you, don't.

Understand that this is not dishonesty. It is not "fronting," as the term is used today to represent deliberately misleading behavior. Instead, it is a masking of emotions, largely due to a fear of dealing with something with which we have little or no experience: feelings. This is not to say we are incapable of expressing extreme sensitivity to emotions, but for many men, emotional vulnerability is expressed in degrees of masculine pride.

The funny thing is, men know the value of feelings. We apply them daily to competitive pursuits: sports, work, or anything else which enhances our worth and elevates our self-esteem. These are strong, positive expressions of a man's emotional side. Women are often puzzled by a man's inability to transfer those positive emotional energies and expressions to their relationship. And even when we are reciting how much we care, it is sometimes difficult for our wives to know if we mean it. They often wonder, Is it real, or are we simply in the mood for love?

Deep down inside, a man wishes he were free to express how he feels. But many times his emotional immaturity leaves him completely unable to adequately handle verbal expressions of intimacy. For some men, it is very difficult to trust feelings, afraid that if they loosen their tongue, they will release what is in their heart. Whereas it may be natural for a man to focus his raw aggression and adrenaline toward a target that requires capturing, often he is left in the dark concerning what to do when confronted by an enemy who lives on the inside: his fear of failure and feelings of inadequacy. Yet if he fails to properly respond to his emotional signals, he will most likely end up doing damage to himself and those around him.

Getting a Handle on Emotions

There are negative and positive emotions, good and bad ones that we must learn to manage—channeling them, so to speak, in the proper direction. We don't always know what to do with love and joy, and most of us have no idea what to do with fear, anger, sorrow, and pride. All these emotions live inside you, underneath the skin, working either negative or positive results in you.

Take fear, for example. It is because of fear most of us wear a mask, and are missing out on the one thing we desire most in life: intimacy. That is, we want to be known, to be loved, and to be accepted for who we are, in spite of our tendencies to fall short of the mark. Have you ever wondered why you are afraid for anyone to discover you harbor deep anxieties about certain deficiencies in your life? It's due to fear. But fear alone is neither a bad nor a destructive emotion. *How you handle it* will determine its influence upon your life.

Fear ought to become your servant. It should sound the alarm when you find yourself floating amidst a sea of danger, or when your path is obscured by darkness. The adrenaline it emits can give you unbelievable strength to rise up and overcome the problem. More than that, it can stimulate you into rightfully recognizing the holy presence and the awesome power of the omnipotent God. But if fear conquers you, you'll always feel like a coward, unable to confront the problem. Remember, "God has not given us a spirit of fear, but of power and of love and of a sound mind" (2 Timothy 1:7).

Similarly, sorrow is God's way of allowing us to feel what He feels because of the cruel acts of sin and the pain of men. It prompts us to grieve and release the anxiety born of a personal loss or to respond with empathy to the hurts of someone else. But growing up is learning what we ought to feel sorrow over. As an adolescent, I remember a kid whose dad would slap him when he cried, and keep slapping him until he stopped. The father wanted to "make him a man." He is now an adult. And sadly, he never cries for anything. Instead, he wears a mask. And I wonder if he has ever really become a man.

You see, if a man is someone mature, then it seems reasonable that a real man is someone who can feel emotion and deal with it in a mature way. To pretend the emotion doesn't exist is immature. To hide it or not deal with it seems juvenile. Satan takes advantage of a man's inability to manage his emotions properly. Anger unchecked will lead from arguments to bitterness, malice, and hatred. Rather than learning the mature response of forgiveness, unchecked anger can destroy a man.

Instead of allowing anger's natural progression to set its course, we should use anger as an opportunity to respond appropriately. If a friend of yours knew you had a problem with anger, he could help you face the challenge of learning to turn it into a weapon for fighting against the devil. Again, *anger is a natural emotion designed by God, but He instructs us to feel it without being victimized by it.* "Be angry and do not sin: do not let the sun go down on your wrath, nor give place to the devil," it says in Ephesians 4:26,27.

Along the same lines, a man who cannot deal with his emotions properly will become either frustrated or proud. The frustrated man will lash out at other people, driving away those closest to him. The proud man will wear on others. In both cases, the men will end their lives without any significant relationships.

Pride is the most deceptive emotion of all, developed by those who somehow come to believe that they achieved their success by their own ingenuity, hard work, and talent. They are, in their own minds, the masters of their fate and the captains of their soul. Sometimes a man becomes so proud he begins to believe his own front-page stories. I thought I was just being confident when I said I was going to make it on my own. But once I found success, I actually believed I did it on my own. That's pride, and it's deadly. I had to learn how to handle success, or my own pride would have destroyed me.

Managing Emotions

Have you ever said to yourself, "I don't need anyone"? You may believe that in your mind, but your heart knows better. It's just a mask we wear. However, it all starts to get better when we care enough for someone, including ourselves, to want to make a change. I have discovered that most men are willing to allow God to change them.

Brothers can help in this process. When we allow others into our lives, and risk sharing honest emotions with them, we are freed up to feel things for other people. Without a few men to whom you can trust your inner soul, it is very difficult to learn the rudiments of managing emotions and developing genuine relationships.

Ask yourself these questions: If you could see your ways and read your emotional meters, what sort of person would you see? What words would you use to characterize your negative traits in need of treatment or transformation? Ask your wife or a couple of your closest friends to help you in identifying areas within your character which would impede your progress toward becoming the best you can be. Write them down. Then pray about the things you have learned from loved ones and discovered through your study of yourself, asking the Holy Spirit to assist you in addressing those areas.

It's scary, but allowing yourself to *feel*, being honest about your feelings, and allowing others into your life are the first steps toward becoming a mature man of God.

6
Men Are
Like Turtles

Take a look at the anatomy of a turtle for a moment. On the outside is an almost impenetrable coating. The reason why the covering is so hard and tightly sealed is because of the presence of deadly predators desiring to sample the tender morsels housed inside. The hard shell protects the turtle—nothing can get through it.

In many ways, a man is much like a turtle. Inside we are naturally soft, sensitive, and vulnerable. But we choose to construct a tough outer covering for the purpose of protecting ourselves from potential predators. That doesn't change what's really inside, but it does change other people's perceptions. A shell keeps people at a distance. Like a mask, it helps hide our identity.

In order to find out who the man is on the inside, one would have to be able to get through that tough exterior. You've heard the expression, "What you see is what you get." It's often not true. What you see is what the guy *wants you to see,* but it isn't necessarily the real man.

Turtles and Trust

Each man is different. Like the turtle, men have a small opening to their inner selves that shuts tight the instant the outer perimeter is breached. It's like a security system, shutting others out in order to protect them from danger and pain. Emotionally, most men have a low threshold for pain. So contrary to what you may have heard, a man can be easily hurt and is quick to retreat. Trust is not one of his strong suits because it allows others access to his life, and thereby creates the *possibility* of getting hurt.

What do you do if you're a turtle? It's tough. You're going to have to make a decision to crawl out of that shell, or at least give someone else access to the inside. It will mean making yourself vulnerable to pain—something none of us wants. But there is no other way to experience true love and fellowship.

The space between a man and others is often carefully measured. Like the turtle, a man generally keeps himself at a safe distance. Yet for his emotional and psychological health, he needs the closeness that comes from intimacy. According to Dr. Dean Ornish, a clinical professor of medicine and nationally known author, researchers have demonstrated a correlation between loneliness and an impaired immune system. Study after study has demonstrated that people who feel lonely and isolated have three to five times the rate of premature death and disease, compared to those who have a sense of connection and community, love and intimacy. So while we think we're protecting ourselves by becoming isolated, we're actually hurting ourselves.

The battles of life are easier to win and the problems less formidable when faced in the company of a friend. Yet men are reluctant to allow a relationship to go beyond the surface due to a lack of trust. Before a turtle will crawl out of his shell, he has to trust that something will not hurt him. A stranger can spell trouble if you're not careful. That is why a man learns to hide his face behind a mask and focus discussions that beg for personal details away from himself.

Trusting in the Lord

Remember the goal of the Christian man: *We want to reflect the Lord Jesus.* The man is "the image and the glory of God," according to 1 Corinthians 11:7. As the glory of a light shines only as bright as the holder through which it is conducted, the illumination of God's radiance gets brighter only as we get better at presenting ourselves as instruments of His glory. No matter how much wattage a bulb has, if it is dirty, the light from it is going to be diminished. If you are hiding yourself inside a hardened shell, you are keeping God from displaying Himself through your life.

Take a look at the brilliance of His glory through you. If you have fathered children, how are you doing as a dad? Can your kids see the love of Jesus reflected in your care? If you are married, what grade do you give yourself as a husband? Does your wife see the tender touch of God in your behavior toward her? Are you afraid to ask her to grade you? As a son, how would your parents rate you? Do they see you honoring them with your words and actions? As a friend, how do you rate? Do those closest to you see the Lord in your life?

I asked myself those questions a few years ago. I realized I was hiding His glory beneath a mask, behind a shell, and it resulted in my isolation from people. God couldn't shine clearly through me; I was too well hidden. Then it occurred to me that if God was looking for a man who would be the shaper of the next generation, the example-setter to those in my world, I would have to give Him total access, make Him Lord in all areas of my life.

Think of it this way: If God were coming into the world in human form as a little boy *today* instead of 2000 years ago, and He needed an earthly stepfather to be the maker of the man and the shaper of His maleness, would He have selected you? I find it fascinating that the Almighty chose Joseph to guard His only begotten Son. Imagine what kind of man Joseph must have been. When he was betrothed to Mary, and they were soon to be married, she went away for three months and came back home pregnant. For all practical purposes, they were already married—the betrothal time was simply a chance for both young people to prove themselves pure, and Mary was clearly pregnant. Joseph knew they had never had sex, yet his fiancée was with child. What would you have done?

Most men, hurt, would have been ready to explode! But do you know what Joseph did? He *trusted* in the Lord. He cared so much for Mary that he considered her condition first. You see, according to Jewish law, Mary was guilty of adultery and supposed to be stoned to death. For her protection, Joseph decided to divorce her quietly, so as to keep Mary's trouble as private as possible.

You may wonder, "If he loved her so much, why didn't he just *marry* her quietly?" The answer is because of his devoutness. Joseph honored God above his own desires and ego. He loved Mary and didn't want to hurt her, but at the same time he knew that marrying an adulteress would bring judgment onto himself. So Joseph decided to secretly give her a writ of divorce, in order to cover her alleged capital crime and yet maintain his own integrity before God. This is an incredible man!

I don't believe I could have done what Joseph did—I probably would have taken a holiday from ration and reason. But Joseph listened to God and did the right thing. And when the Lord called him to wed Mary anyway, he continued to trust and went through the marriage ceremony. *That* is the kind of man I want to be at my house. I want to have so much trust in God that, even when things appear to have blown up, I can still feel confident He is in charge.

My wife is not perfect, but she is God's wonderful gift to me. I have blown up over things she has done that were far less grievous than being impregnated by someone else. But Joseph did just the right thing. Rather than hide in his shell, he trusted God. When he received a message from an angel telling him that the life of the baby was threatened and they would have to get up in the middle of the night and flee to the country of Egypt, Joseph got up and left. Would you have done that? And if you woke your wife early one morning to say, "God came to me and told me . . ." would she ask, "Where did He catch up with you, on the back nine of the golf course?" Or would she know you were telling the truth because she has seen your trust in God over time?

What a marvelous covering Mary had! Joseph protected and cared for her, trusting in her and in God, though he knew it could lead to tremendous hurt. In fact, it might have—there could very well have been people in Bethlehem who thought he had disgraced himself by marrying a pregnant girl. But Joseph trusted his wife and his God. I want to be like Joseph. I want God to use me as an instrument of His blessing in my house for my wife and children. The critical question is, "Am I prepared to trust others?"

Opening a Trust Account

Was it difficult for me to change and begin to open myself up to others? Yes. I'm really not certain why, but it was. Maybe that's because of my background—I wasn't raised to trust others. I learned to trust myself. If you are distrusting of others, a psychologist might say it is because your heart, as a child, was pierced with the deep pain of broken promises. Maybe you suffered from feeling misunderstood. Or your reticence may have come from having felt the deliberate kiss of deceit from the smiling lips of a so-called friend more than once.

In my case, for numerous reasons, somewhere along the way I developed a lack of trust in other people. And I believe that is the primary explanation why many men hesitate to commit to being fully known by anyone. *A lack of trust is the main obstacle to friendships.* I had to open a "trust account" with another man—to begin making "trust deposits" into our friendship account, sharing my life with him and trusting he would respect my privacy and not hurt me. Opening that account took a long time. The account started small—a few pennies of trust. But over time that account built up, the trust accumulated, and eventually I found myself trusting my friend completely.

Allow me to ask you a question: Do you trust me? Your response would probably be, "I don't know you." You're right, but who do you know enough to trust? An alternative answer could be, "Why should I trust you?" To that I would say, "Because I have not done anything that would give you a reason not to trust me." Unfortunately, I am judged in light of your own experience. You've probably been burned before, so you're not interested in hurrying into a new, potentially painful relationship. You don't want to trust someone and get hurt again. That is why trust must be built over time—but I can't earn it unless you give me a chance to try.

Brother, we are all created in the image of God and embody some aspect of His attributes and characteristics. God places a high premium on our worth, demonstrating His commitment to us on Calvary. That alone is reason enough to give me the benefit of the doubt until I prove otherwise. The strength of trust is security. If I lack confidence in someone, it is because I am not secure with him. In reality, there is only one place where I can find complete security, and only one Person in whom perfect trust exists. My lack of trust in another person is not the problem—my lack of trust in *God* is the problem. If I trust in the Lord, I can open myself up to another person and risk getting hurt. But if I can't even trust God, then I can never truly be fully known by anyone but God.

The truth is, sooner or later someone is going to let me down. It is a function of the frailties of mankind in general. But man's failure doesn't mean I can never trust again. I trust God, even when friends fail. I once heard the refrain to a song that correctly identifies the only sure foundation upon which I can safely stand. Quoting the psalmist, the words say, "When I need shelter, when I need a friend, I go to the Rock."

For a man to build trust, he needs to do two things: Trust in an unfailing God, and begin opening a trust account with another man, a friend. Both these things are necessary. We can't just trust in ourselves, for we need others. God made us with a desire for relationships. Nor can we trust merely in others, for the Bible reminds us that men are limited and unpredictable, fragile and fading. The Scriptures say, "Cursed is the man that trusts in man and makes flesh his arm of strength, whose heart departs from the Lord." When it comes to personal fulfillment and satisfaction, history has proven over and over again that the answer to all of our needs is found only in the Lord. Neither man's wealth, nor his power, nor his influence is sufficient when it comes to solving life's most critical problems. And yet most of us spend the majority of our time in pursuit of those things, hoping success will somehow fill the gaps that we feel in our lives because of loneliness. But fame and finances will never be enough. At the end of life, all that matters is friends and family.

I have sat beside men who were facing the end of life, and none of them spoke of the money they made. They always wanted to talk about friends. Without friends, without love relationships, life becomes a selfish, meaningless gesture. God made us for relationships, and to ignore them is to reject His plan. But you can't develop friends if you're a turtle. It takes trust—trust in God and brothers who are trustworthy.

If you're a turtle, I urge you to begin reading the Old Testament. Look at how God has proven Himself faithful in the past. Surely if He has always upheld His promises in the past, He will do so in the future. Ours is a God you can trust. Look for His hand in your life, and thank Him for all the times He has proven Himself faithful.

Carl Martin, a close friend and confidant from my fellowship, once told me, *"He who can see God's hand in everything, can best leave everything in the hand of God."* Far too often we see God as a Sunday-morning date, or as a part-time friend, instead of as our permanent Provider and the One in whom we trust. Everything He has said, He will do. Learning to trust Him is the first step in learning to take off our masks and cultivating true friendships with others.

7
A New School of Thought

As our Thursday morning fellowship began to grow, I paid particular attention to the kind of men God was directing to the men's meeting. I noted that from out of the world He was continuously introducing into His family a variety of different temperaments and personalities. Many times His choices were radical—they didn't fit in. The rest of us didn't know what to do with a man who was radically different from ourselves.

That made it hard to trust. Often as people surrender their lives to God, they come from all directions and with a lot of baggage. They have a multitude of easily identifiable personal priorities hanging on to their shirttails like frost on the kitchen windowpane.

Unfortunately, even men with baggage can look polished. We soon found our group included polished people pretending to be perfect. Like us, they were men in masks. What do you do when you're committed to a relationship with turtles and masked men? We knew the answer was "develop trust," but how do you develop trust when you can't really get to know them?

The answer, we found, was simple: *Learn to spend time together.*

Spending Time

It ticks me off to see men who are phonies. Why? Because they remind me of myself! Every time I had to face a man I knew was being dishonest, it made me angry. The only way to get over my anger and learn to like the guy was to spend time with him.

At first I resisted—if I already didn't like the guy, I figured I would like him less if I was forced to spend the day listening to him. But the opposite happened. The more I spent time, the more I got to know the man's heart. And the more I understood why he acted the way he did. A bad childhood can make a man protective. Damaged relationships turn a man into a turtle. A lousy marriage is hidden behind the mask of possessions, in order to help the man feel successful at something.

As we began spending significant time with one another, the barriers dropped between us and trust developed. Gradually we settled into comfortable relationships with one another, learning to be what God has always been to us—a lover of souls.

One brother came believing he had a special standing in our group due to his parents' faithful membership in the local church. If you asked him, he would tell you he had always been close to God. That man hid himself behind the mask of arrogance and his family's religious history. But inside he was hurting—desperate to be known, but unwilling to open himself up. It took a great investment of time before he would allow anyone to know his heart.

Another man came like someone soaking wet and glad to be out of the rain. He had been a wee bit out of control, and knew that he barely escaped total demise at the hands of his own devices. But now that he was in Christ, he saw everyone else in the church as nothing but self-serving, carnal, hypocritical sinners. His criticisms covered over his own feelings of inadequacy, and his past indulgence into drugs had simply been a way to kill his internal pain. Over time, we saw the man change—but only after he saw our commitment to him as a friend, regardless of his sarcasm and negativity.

Some men entered the fellowship with long faces, feeling unloved and of little value. Others came with a spiritual swagger, symbols of accomplishments and worldly successes pinned to their suits like a backstage pass at a concert. They were a diverse group, but they all had one thing in common: the mask. They needed to learn trust in order to feel like they belonged. And trust only came as they spent time with others, appreciating the brothers' diversity and learning to trust God's grand design in creating different people.

We were all family. And we all experienced God's transforming power. He helped us see each other as new men, a new creation, with each individual valuable and a work of God in progress.

Getting the Focus Off Me

Because of our commitment to one another, we began to believe in a new school of thought. Rather than the church being a mass of individuals, we started to see one another as family. As brothers in Christ, we *desired* to spend time with one another, supporting each other. This was an entirely new way of thinking for most of us, and we started to get a glimpse of how the Lord was going to use our meetings to shape not only our individual lives, but also the entire family of God.

We used to keep a big imaginary dumpster parked right next to our meeting space. The men wanted to get rid of as much of the garbage they brought into the meetings as possible, washing their lives thoroughly with the water of the Word. Remember, our meeting together was not a Bible study for discussing doctrine, but a place where we allowed His Word into our lives for our personal benefit. It was challenging because we were exploring our walk with God constantly, and regularly checking with each other to see how we were growing spiritually.

All of us started taking off our masks and seeing the faces on our brothers. We slowly began to feel we were getting to know each other. We would explore our struggles through the Scriptures, asking ourselves what we would have done in a brother's situation, or how would we have responded if we had been in his place.

That sort of discussion moved our perspectives away from our own troubles and onto the greater picture of how we were all growing together in the Lord. We figured if we could not walk with one or two brothers we already knew, we were never going to be able to walk with the rest of His family. In my view, God's crowning achievement is the bringing together of diverse men in order to create a new man—and a new family. Instead of competing with and opposing each other, we were compounding our gifts for the kingdom. Rather than being divided, we were united in Christ.

God has purposely tied our spiritual growth to our willingness to cooperate with His plan. Rather than sitting alone and trying to be holy, we found ourselves growing in grace as we opened ourselves to one another. God's multifaceted, diverse, and multidimensional family was determining to walk together. In doing so, we were able to observe some incredible victories.

Following the Example of Jesus

Jesus once told His followers, "If anyone wants to sue you and take away your tunic, let him have your cloak also. And whoever compels you to go one mile, go with him two. Give to him who asks you, and from him who wants to borrow from you do not turn away" (Matthew 5:40-42). In other words, Jesus' entire doctrine regarding relationships is a reorientation of how we think. He wants us to trust.

The Lord wants us to trust Him. He wants us to be open enough to trust one another. In time, we'll even gain discernment in trusting strangers. It is a new school of thought. Rather than distrusting people, the more we love God, the more we bank on Him, and that makes us willing to take a chance on others. In trusting other men, our lives change and grow. We saw that evidence of this put into play in the lives of one of our brothers.

Late one evening, evangelist Tom Skinner got onto an elevator in a New York City office complex and immediately faced a young and desperate thief. He became a victim of a robbery at gunpoint. After demanding Tom's wallet, the thief was informed by Tom that there was also an ATM machine in the building, where he could get some additional cash if he had time to accompany his victim. Startled and somewhat leery, the robber proceeded to the bank with Tom to make a withdrawal.

While counting the money out to him, Tom interrupted the gunman's gleeful thoughts with the statement, "I can give you this money because my Father will replace it. But you know that you don't have to live like this, don't you?"

"Live like what?" the young man retorted. "I've got your money!"

"Evidently you don't know who you are," Tom explained. "Your Father is rich in houses and in land."

"You don't know what you're talking about," the thief insisted. "My dad's a bum!"

"No, it's you who doesn't understand," Tom pressed. "You've got a Father who loves and cares for you."

"What? If my father had not dumped us like a sack of old garbage while we were kids, I would have had a chance to make a life for myself. But now I have a wife, two kids, and a sick mother to take care of. It's all on me, and I can't find a job, so don't tell me about my shiftless father."

Patiently and with his countenance full of the peace of God, Tom responded, "Young man, I don't mean your earthly father. Your *heavenly* Father realizes that our parents here on earth might fail in their responsibility, but He has designed His own personal plan for your life. Son, what you don't know can hurt you far more than what you do know." Then, with the words of one who appeared to be gazing up into glory, he molded in the mind of that young thief the invisible face of his heavenly Father. Tom encouraged the man who had robbed him to put his trust in God. Standing in the darkened lobby of an office building near midnight, Tom led a trembling, lost lad to a new life in Christ.

Tom didn't trust in money—in fact, he gave it away. He didn't trust in security cameras. He put his trust in God, and shared that fact with his enemy. In doing so, he made that man a friend . . . and ushered him into the kingdom of God.

8

I Need to Be Encouraged

A key ingredient that we found to make our meetings successful was *encouragement.* As we would gather in a restaurant and begin talking about our lives, the Word of God was always there to help us understand our situations better and offer us prescriptions for improvement. Many times a brother would begin talking about some struggle he was facing, and the rest of the group would encourage him with reminders of how God has worked, either in history or in their own lives.

"As iron sharpens iron, so one man sharpens another," it says in Proverbs. So it was with us—as we studied God's Word and applied it to our lives, each of us became a better tool in the hands of the Lord. For example, one guy was lamenting a painful failure in his professional life, but as we talked about it, it became clear the mysterious hand of God was using that circumstance to guide him toward victory. What looked like a disaster was actually just a growing pain. Another brother was crowing about the solid successes he had experienced. But the more we learned about his life overall, it became obvious the price he had paid in time away from his loved ones negated much of his gain.

When men gather together to share their hearts, listening to the diverse encounters of each brother, the immensity of God and His overall plan become more clear. As each of us listened to others talk, we discerned spiritual principles that applied to our own lives.

Seeing the Hand of God

What became clear to all of us in the fellowship is that God's ways are not our ways. He is a patient, loving Lord, who stays with us even when we mess up. He always seeks what is best for us, even though we cannot always understand why events unfold as they do. Yet over time, everyone who loves the Lord can see the hand of God at work in his life.

That's why it is so uplifting to share your life with a group of men. I might arrive for the meeting discouraged one morning, having had bad news or a struggle in the family, but as I see how God is working in the lives of others, I am inspired to trust Him all over again.

One never knows what God is up to in the midst of our individual struggles. You may think it is easy to arrive at a prognosis of your condition based upon one fact or another, and you might be tempted to put God on a time line. In other words, you begin to think to yourself, "If victory is not at hand by midnight, I'm finished, it's too late." But in doing so, you miss the chance to see the Lord work. God is not bound by our circumstances. Even if we get a little off on our timing and miss great opportunities to get ahead, God is not bothered. He remains with us. The Lord can be fully trusted. His ways are not our ways.

Time after time we were encouraged by seeing God work in the lives of the brothers.

Dennis was very successful in his business but a failure in his marriage. He worked endless hours to provide for his family, but he was robbing his wife's emotional and spiritual needs to pay for her economic and prestige needs. While Dennis was busy running his business, a member of his church was busy seducing his wife. He was devastated. We walked through that tough time with our brother, giving him courage in the midst of his crisis and supporting him in prayer. From this painful lesson, we learned the importance of priorities—every one of us had to consider the time we were investing in our own marriage. I cannot over emphasize the positive effect upon our spiritual development that has come from spending time and practicing the principles of walking together.

Putting the "En" in Courage

Several years ago I had hit a slight lull in my own life. After completing a busy spring and summer, I was starting to wonder about the effectiveness and significance of my endeavors. Was God getting as much out of me as He desired, or was I holding out on Him? At the same time we were having some challenges with one of our daughters, and that had impacted the entire family. On top of that, I had a few blows to my pocketbook, which made me sensitive to the fact that nobody seemed to turn off a light or put leftovers in the refrigerator. No matter how often Bunny and I spoke to our children about it, they didn't remember it until they were being reminded again. And besides, according to whichever one you were addressing, they weren't the guilty party anyway. What started as a small series of struggles began to turn into one giant battle with the enemy.

Sometimes you can do all the things you think are right, only to see your energy and the resources you've expended go to waste. I was angry, nervous, and not feeling very appreciated. However, I had noticed that since I had been walking with other men, the Lord would often use a friend to remind me of my "Help."

One evening, we heard the doorbell ring. Bunny and I were sitting in the living room after engaging in an afternoon of problem solving, and we both sighed at the unexpected interruption. "Now who could that be?" I wondered out loud. It was too late in the day for a salesman, and the kids were all inside for the evening, so when I peered out the window I received a huge shock. It way my dear friend Tom Skinner, who just happened to be in town away from his home in Washington, DC.

I hurriedly opened the door, and he greeted me with his customary, "What's going on there, young man?" Tom had a way of making one feel special just by saying hello, and I always cherished our times together. On many occasions he had ministered deeply to me, my family, and my friends. His sacrifice for us was not something that could have been natural; it had to come from the Lord.

"What are you doing here in Los Angeles?" I asked him incredulously.

"My plane just got in from New Zealand," he responded. "I had a few hours layover and wanted to see two of my favorite people before leaving again." He was one of the busiest men on the planet.

The distance from the Los Angeles airport to our home is approximately 40 miles, and Tom must have passed many friends who would have been honored to spend a few precious minutes alone with him.

Briefly, I thought back to the weekend when Bunny and I took the family to New York. On that Friday night she and I were obligated to attend a fundraiser. Tom volunteered to chaperone and entertain our three small children for the evening. Together they painted the town. Our children had the time of their lives.

For such an extraordinary person, Tom had an ability to do ordinary things naturally. I learned a great deal while watching him. For instance, one afternoon while he was teaching on the subject of love at the Christian Entertainers' Bible Study, a young woman in attendance shared how she had been hurt so much that she had no love left for anyone. Tom asked the audience, "How many of you have ever prayed for more love? 'God,' you said, 'I need more love in my heart for people.' Raise your hands if you've ever prayed that prayer." Everyone in the room raised their hands. "That's a dumb prayer," he chuckled. We all looked stunned, so he continued by saying, "The Bible says in 1 John that God is what? Love! And that same God lives right there in your heart. So if the Lord resides in your heart, what must you be filled with? That's right: love.

"The Spirit," he reminded us, "lives in you, and His fruit is love, joy, peace, patience, kindness, meekness, goodness, faithfulness, and self-control. All that God is, lives inside of you." Then he paused before finally stating, "Perhaps it is not more love you need. Maybe God simply needs more of you." That is the kind of teacher Tom was, laced throughout with words of encouragement.

So on the night of his visit with Bunny and me, his ministry to us was no less impactful. I cannot even say for certain what we discussed, but as usual, sprinkled amidst our moments of fellowship, Bunny and I peppered him with myriad questions. When he rose to leave, it was the end of a good day. We walked with him to the door, and I noticed the sound of an idling automobile engine. Instantly it occurred to me that I had been hearing that engine idling for quite some time. Opening the door, I looked around the corner of our house and in the driveway was a yellow cab. Bunny and I were flabbergasted! "Tom, we didn't know you had a taxi waiting. Send him away and we'll take you back to the airport."

Tom wouldn't hear of it. "No, I'm fine. I just wanted to see you for a short spell. You guys don't need to make that drive this late." Then he left. As his taxi pulled away from the front of our home, I thought gladly, "My brother." He lives on the other side of the country, and he took the time to come visit us when the Spirit nudged him. That's commitment. That's encouragement.

Kingdom-Centered Relationships

God often anticipates our needs even before we call Him. During his visit with us, Tom insightfully interrupted our subjective personal points of view and interjected His own objective overview without knowing that we were struggling with deep issues. At the end of the day, our troubles had lost their importance. We just needed the encouragement and input of someone who did not have a personal agenda to advance, a reputation to protect, or a need to be right. God simply tells us to pray, "Thy kingdom come," then asks, "Does this discussion have anything to do with it?"

My brother Tom came from a great distance, going out of his way and at his own expense to encourage us. He left a lasting legacy in our hearts that said, "You are important to me." While I was worrying about my circumstances, God was thinking about my soul.

The one thing that stands out in my mind from that night is this: Tom was not thinking about practicing any principles; he was just being my brother. In the process he gave to us the most valuable things he had to give: his time and encouragement. Think about someone who has impacted your life in that manner through an unusual extension of kindness to you. Why did he or she do it?

Was it to get something from you? Or was it God's love on trial?

In our group, we want to *be* the Word of God to our brothers. We want to take off our masks and find a brother with whom we can be honest. Then we want to encourage that man with our love and service.

My friend Tom once told me that in order for us to experience a foretaste of Glory, God desires to live His life through us with no help from us. As we allow that to happen, we draw closer to Him and one another. That is the reason we need each other: to encourage one another to practice letting and allowing God to be God in us.

9
A Place to Be Real

On any given Thursday morning, there are no superspiritual dynamos present in our men's group (unless you count Jesus). Instead you'll find several cautious midgets masquerading as giants, waiting until they know for certain it is safe to remove their masks. In time we each discover that when the covers finally come off, the mighty ministry of the Holy Spirit is unleashed. We hear from God and His words are always striking, designed to respond to our individual needs in the midst of an outpouring of His wisdom. It is awe-inspiring to watch the Lord use ordinary people in the midst of extraordinary problems—a testimony to God's power.

Afterward, you can look around the room and see groups of honest men weeping. You could say that was the only good thing about more than a few of them, because it turns out that some of them are greedy, adulterers, drug users, liars, embezzlers, coveters, fornicators, masturbators, and chronic procrastinators. In fact, they are all sinners saved by grace. Interestingly, some of these same men were politicians, corporate executives, newscasters, professional athletes, preachers, teachers, and men going to work every day as heads of families and leaders in the community. But healing for them was on the way, because hiding who they were was no longer an option.

A Private Dressing Room

Recently Clay, a pastor from Portland, had this to say about walking with a few brothers: "The greatest source of my spiritual growth can be attributed to the Thursday morning fellowship. It brought an accountability into my life that I had never had before. I can recall an instance that happened one Sunday evening as my wife and I were about to enter the church building. I had just made some stupid remark, and my wife was wiping tears from her eyes. Just then, one of the brothers from the fellowship approached us and noticed her tears. He spoke privately as he passed by: 'Brother, your wife's lights are out—fix them.' His meaning was clear: 'Comfort your wife.' I suppose most men would have told him to mind his own business, but he and I had been walking together for over a year, and I had given him the right to speak into my life. Turning to my wife, I realized it was my words and my attitude that had hurt her. In a direct way, my wife benefited from the relationship this brother and I had."

Contrary to popular opinion, God is not as impressed with us as we are with ourselves. He knows what is in every man's heart. And He desires to undress us in order that He may bless us with a new wardrobe made from the nature of His Son. The Apostle Paul described his life this way: "For I know that in me . . . nothing good dwells; for to will is present with me, but how to perform what is good I do not find" (Romans 7:18). Later, in that same letter to the Romans, he emphasizes, "But put on the Lord Jesus Christ, and make no provision for the flesh, to fulfill its lusts" (Romans 13:14).

As Christian men, we are called to change the garments of our lives. We are to take off the old man and put on the new. In the process, we need a private room in which to dress. We need a place where we can take off the old clothes and be fitted for the new ones without feeling uncomfortable and foolish. Our old ideas of what looks good must be questioned by those who care about us. Until we can get it right, changing styles, like a changing life, sometime sets us up for ridicule and could be an embarrassment to our friends and family if we make poor choices.

But while walking together, we pray for one another's weaknesses and conceal each other's nakedness. Always cognizant of the Scripture which says, "Love covers a multitude of sins [or faults]," we support one another in private. Whether together in a meeting or alone in a one-on-one encounter, we are called to challenge each other and spur each other on to greater love and good works.

Earning the Right to Confront

Walter was one arrogant man. He was proud of his accomplishments in life and wanted everybody to know it. But inside, he was afraid of failing. Guys like that often make themselves out to be something they're not. They end up spending way too much money in order to project a "lifestyle of the rich and famous," of which he was neither. But he believed if you don't project a certain pompousness in this world, other people may not give to you the respect you feel you deserve. Walter was thinking, "If I don't act important, others will walk all over me."

One day he met some brothers in the fellowship who had experienced great success, but you would have never known it because of their humility. He discovered he didn't need to put a facade on the outside; he just needed some authority on the inside. Walter had to develop that spiritual posture which says, "I'm somebody because I'm with God."

Have you ever tried to get into a restricted area, like a private reception for a dignitary, and all you had to say was "I'm with him" and immediately the door swung open? In the same way, Walter found out that he did not have to kowtow to anybody. He is with God! We are who we are by God's grace. Consequently, we can be real, powerful, and exert influence upon our world without becoming arrogant. But Walter would never have learned that lesson were it not for the safety of our private gatherings.

"We need to practice being bold enough," we would tell each other, "to speak the word of life into each other's hearts irrespective of receptivity." In other words, we were committed to telling the truth. Even if it makes the brother mad at the time, and he tries to walk away from the relationship, we tell him the truth. He'll be back, and he will be better. As King Solomon put it, "Faithful are the wounds of a friend. But the kisses of an enemy are deceitful" (Proverbs 27:6).

We declared ourselves to be that brother who encourages, exhorts, confronts, and inspires others to get off their own well-worn paths of personal pursuits and consistently work out the meaning of seeking first the kingdom of God.

Of course, in order to do this, we had to earn the right to be heard. And we did that by proving to one another the strength of our commitment, demonstrating love and concern for however long it took, and by being there for a brother unconditionally. Each of us was devoted to speaking the truth and not walking away because of another man's stubbornness or his shortcomings. I earned the right to talk with my brothers, and they earned the right to confront me.

Mutual Imperfections

In our presence there is no need for anyone to put on a mask. The Scripture says that *all* have sinned and come short of God's glory, and that includes me. But we must be honest about our spiritual condition. You don't have to fake it. I know how it is. Every now and then you just want to relax and let your hair down. We do not feel like doing the right thing all the time. You're not alone. You want to take a spiritual nap and give your flesh a holiday.

Get real! Our enemy doesn't sleep, nor does he ever go on a vacation. We cannot afford a lapse in our attentiveness to temptation. If we do, we may wake up and find that he has ruined our lives. The Bible says that Satan wants to ruin us—he comes only to steal, kill, and destroy (John 10:10).

That's why each man needs a place to be transparent and to be confronted. When we think about our own weaknesses, we ought to remember our brother and cut him some slack, but not cut him loose. Consider the advice of Paul: "Brethren, if a man be overtaken in a fault, ye which are spiritual, restore such a one in the spirit of meekness; considering thyself, lest thou also be tempted" (Galatians 6:1 KJV). What is always interesting to me is how much it appears to be *fact* that the hardest and least tolerant people on smokers are ex-smokers. Stop being so judgmental unless you are prepared to have God judge you based upon the same scale of perfection!

One of the things we learned in our fellowship was that each man should be open enough to hear a word of caution from a brother in the face of fleshly cravings, even when he doesn't want to hear it. Remember, sex is not the only temptation of the flesh—everything alive is growing and multiplying itself. If you are not growing and multiplying your spiritual life, you are letting it die. A non-Christian is a dead man walking. A Christian not growing in the spirit is sleepwalking. Therefore we are not surprised to see one stumble and fall. The goal of our group is to help unearth the best person inside each brother, while defending him from the stagnating effects of personal failures.

Many people seem to get thrown away in this world because they don't measure up. They aren't "successful" in the eyes of men. But we can, by virtue of our love for each other, help draw out the strengths that are being covered up by fear and faults. Men are afraid because life has told them over and over again, "You're not good enough." Yet no one knows how great a man can be if we are not patient enough to look and see the priceless gem God has lodged deep inside him. If I'm walking with a brother, I must take the time to discover the unique treasure God has hidden inside the man. And the body of Christ inherits a gift of enormous value.

Growing Room

Why would anyone go through so much trouble to develop that sort of committed relationship with another brother? First, because he wishes to grow. When you invest in the life of another, you find your own soul climbing higher. Service and selfless love are two of the best tools a man can use in the garden of his life.

Second, you do it because you believe in the body of Christ. *I've personally seen too many Lone Rangers die with their boots on due to their pride and spiritual blindness.* No one was there to warn them of a chink in their spiritual armor, or the cleverly disguised ambush waiting for them just up the road. When you help a man see his error, you may save his life and strengthen the family of God.

Third, you do it out of your love for the Lord. At the end of each day, as I lie in bed and contemplate my life, I realize I'm on this planet for a purpose. God designed and ordained it. He wants me to partner with him in building others up. He expects me to leave a legacy of love among the brothers. And the truth is, I need a brother to help keep me from straying! Even though I enjoy a lifetime of productive activities, if I fail in living His plan for my life, I've missed my real reason for being here.

It doesn't matter how good we may look on the outside, we all are flawed one way or another. I need a make-over—a change of clothes. It starts with me presenting my body as a living sacrifice, holy and acceptable to God. Then I must resist being conformed to this world's system, submit to His Word, and be transformed by the renewing of my mind. That happens best when I've got a place to be real, with men I trust, where I can give attention to a new school of thought and live out my purpose here on this earth.

A friend inspired me with a song he wrote entitled "If You Can Use Anything, Lord, You Can Use Me." In the lyrics of the song he talks about Jesus taking nothing but two fish and five loaves of bread, and using them to feed 5000 people. If God can do a great work with nothing but fish and bread, surely He can use me for some great service. Likewise, the song lyrics lift up the triumph of Moses and the rod he used to open the Red Sea. David used a simple rock to slay Goliath. If the Lord can accomplish such great feats with such simple tools, then surely He can do something great through me. If You can use anything, Lord, You can use me.

The simple truth is that God can use anything, but He desires to use *us*. But first He must prepare us before He positions and empowers each one to be a vessel for His service. And He uses other people in the process of that preparation to help shape us as instruments for His glory. When you have a place to be real, you enter that exciting place of knowing you are being sanctified for supernatural service.

10
Coming to Commitment

It was early summer, but because of the drought the dusty gloom of springtime had laid a heavy burden across the weary womb of mother Africa. Larry, then a television reporter for ABC News, now a CBS world news anchor, had volunteered to head a film team commissioned to track the cause of this severe water shortage as it hurtled relentlessly the entire weight of its wrath against the weakened resistance of a continent. Larry was simultaneously set to produce a television special from this footage, slated for airing later in the year. However, long before this adventure was envisioned and our bags were packed, he and I had spent many mornings, afternoons, and days on end, discussing the meaning of brotherly love and the art of putting into place God's formula for practical family living.

Larry was going through a bitter and costly divorce. At the same time he was slowly discovering that God is faithful even when we find ourselves caught in the midst of a crisis of our own making. Larry was in the process of becoming a brother.

Being in Africa would give him a chance to get his mind off his troubles. I had hoped that his seeing the unbearable suffering thrust upon a people too worn down to deflect the stifling glare of a faceless foe, and helping them to fight for their survival, would be exactly the diversion he needed to gain a fresh outlook on life.

Glandion Carney, who was leading this mission, I met a few years earlier while he was still a director with Youth for Christ. He and I were just beginning to invest time in getting to know each other through the business of ministry. We had already experienced worshiping and socializing together. But as you know, it is often in the arena where resources are accumulated and distributed that the difference between friendship and hardship, profit and loss is measured. Our desire was to rise above the common characteristic of self-concern, and to learn the ways of walking together.

Often we had discussed it in theory, but we soon discovered that life will eventually arrange an actual experience for testing the depth of your commitment to one another. As Jesus says, "You cannot serve God and mammon" (Matthew 6:24). Even though you may try to avoid it, one day you will be challenged to choose.

Therefore you should not be surprised to discover how easily one person will trash the reputation of another simply to gain favor in the eyes of his employer, to win over a possible beneficial business contact or friend, or even for the silly purpose of inflating the noteworthiness of his own importance.

Taking a Chance on a Brother

I believe that if you were honest, you would have to admit that at one time you also grappled with the difficult-to-grasp notion of placing someone else before yourself. In fact, to be exact, when I first read Galatians 5:16 ("For all the law is fulfilled in one word even in this, 'you shall love your neighbor as yourself.' "), I had to know you and like you immensely, or else I wouldn't even consider this verse of Scripture. In the real world I knew I would not be at the top of your priority list, especially not as the beneficiary. As the old saying goes, nice guys finish last.

Yet according to the Bible we are at our best only after we have learned how to humble ourselves in the sight of the Lord, esteem others as higher than ourselves, and allow Him to lift us up "in due season."

Consequently, the more I matured in the faith, the more I realized the importance of fellowship with others God might choose to use in the ongoing process of my personal growth. I began to widen my borders and relax the safeguards that shielded me from the deceptiveness of false friends and started to develop an attitude of trust. Larry and Glandion were two of the men with whom I was beginning to spend time. And yet I knew that, like with most men I had met, even their best intentions would offer no guarantee.

Committing to Each Other

The three of us, along with a party of seven others, were on our way to Africa for the purpose of learning as much as we could about the deadly drought and famine which were slowly sapping the land of its strength and ravishing its people. Psyched up in anticipation of our mission, I doubt if I slept more than a total of one hour the entire plane ride. We had one brief layover in Amsterdam before arriving in Nairobi, Kenya, late in the East African afternoon.

After checking into our rooms, we grabbed a quick bite of American cuisine in the snack bar of the hotel. Although the long trip had been grueling, we were much too excited to retire for the evening, so we decided to ask someone for the location of some favorite recreational spot frequented by native inhabitants. We told ourselves that the plan was for us to go and get a feel for the lay of the land. However, I suppose we really just wanted to hang out with the brothers.

According to the directions given us by the concierge, we were within easy walking distance of a very lively spot. For the sake of convenience, the three of us plus one of our other team members hailed a taxi and arrived at our destination approximately five minutes later. Once we disembarked and entered the establishment, we saw that the "hip" café we were told about was nothing more than a colorful but heavily crowded bar, with music blaring from small, distorted speakers stationed in the far corners of the wall. There was also a tiny area, with strobe lights on it, set aside for dancing. It was like being at a bad bar in the States, where locals fill the pub on Friday nights after everybody gets paid.

With darting eyes we carefully surveyed the inhabitants of our surroundings, concluding this was not the place nor the time to be away from our group. Instead of soliciting a cab to take us back to the hotel, we decided to walk in spite of the warnings about crime in the area. It looked safe enough—especially after spotting the brightly lit neon marquee on the front of our hotel. It was evident to us that by utilizing a shorter route through the park, it would take us no more than 10 or 15 minutes at the most to get there.

The night was clear, and this sparsely populated area was filled with picture-perfect groves of large, leafy shrubs and trees. It was very quiet. We leisurely made our way toward the blue-and-white lights outside our living quarters, chatting joyously about the expectations for this trip and tomorrow morning's scheduled first day on the job.

As we occupied ourselves with the romantic ruminations of Africa's past history and potential for its future in the world, we began to hear faint footsteps and shortened breaths approaching fast behind us. Turning rapidly, we saw under the pale glimmer of a quarter moon, the shadowy figures of four or five tall, lanky men heading straight toward us. We picked up our pace, but it was clear to us they were doing the same. We hurriedly settled into a smooth gait while looking back over our shoulders, then quickly shifted into high gear. I could feel sudden panic pounding upon the walls of my pulsating chest as I reached for each new step. I had no idea I could run nearly as well as I did, and Glandion, whose normal pace always appeared to be laid-back, was way out in front of us, his long legs grabbing ground by the chunks. Just like that, we turned a 15-minute walk of pleasure into a 3-minute "run for your life." Urgently I prayed that neither of my friends would fall, because I knew I would be called to respond.

Relying On Others

As I think back on that night, one thing stands out: I am thankful I was not alone, and that we were walking together. The Bible tells us that "a friend loves at all times," not simply when it is convenient or is without risk. Proverbs 17:17 adds, "and a brother is born for adversity." We talked about those verses when we got back to our hotel, but to be completely honest, I was not looking for a testimony to prove it!

It is written that a true brother will not leave you to fight your battles alone, and I believe the Bible's report. When Jonathan took off his robe, his sword, and his bow, handing them to David, he was declaring, "I've got your back. Your fight is my fight! Your victories will be my victories and your defeats, mine" (1 Samuel 18:4). In the New Testament, Paul consistently refers to the Christian's life as a "walk." He exhorts us to "walk in the light," "walk in love," and "walk by faith." To walk that way with a brother requires commitment. Not just a simple, easy commitment, but a firm, strong commitment.

As you no doubt have discovered for yourself, the journey down here is no easy walk. Job, an "upright and perfect man, one who feared God and habitually avoided evil," informs us that, "A man who is born of woman is of few days and full of trouble" (Job 14:1). *This life is not easy, but the trip is made infinitely less difficult when undertaken with a brother.* Of course, the devil knows that too, and he uses our pride and self-conceit to create dissension within our ranks, in order to keep us isolated.

I've seen it happen time after time. Stan wants to be Geoffrey's friend. But Geoffrey wants Stan to change his personality and become like him, believe and think like him, vote like him, even dress and talk like him. Stan cannot, for he is having too much difficulty just being himself. In order to behave as brothers, both must strive to become more like Christ. One must not become like the other; each must die to self and forsake the pull of personal propaganda.

None of us have it all together, no matter how good we look. All of us have major flaws in our character. Loving one another is the grease that keeps the wheel of God's will for our lives in motion. If we can break free from our old ways of thinking, take a chance, trust another man, and begin walking together, we can be more than friends—we can be brothers in the Lord.

A Man's Pride

I'll never forget racing through that park, fearing for my life. Yet at the same time, I knew that if I stumbled my brothers would be right there beside me, trying to protect me. My pride was set aside, and I could think about only one thing: survival. Fear will do that to you. But like most things, it requires an extreme situation before most men are willing to surrender their pride and admit they need help.

For example, two of the brothers in our group, Peter and George, are members of the same church and regular social associates. Peter, a hard worker and a proud man, got laid off from his job. Almost three months had gone by since his last paycheck, and his failure to pay the mortgage was heading into its second month. Martha, his loving wife and mother of their three children, was not employed and started to feel a pang of insecurity. But if you looked at Peter from the outside, you would never have known anything was wrong. He looked good, didn't complain, and didn't let on to any of us that he was facing difficult times.

But at a church prayer meeting, Peter's wife shared their growing crisis with her close friend Wanda, who happened to be George's wife. Wanda in turn related to her husband the story of Peter and Martha's financial problems. Before she knew it, George was on the phone with Peter. "How are you doing, partner?" he asked.

"Fine," Peter said, trying to sound upbeat.

"That's great." Then, after a little more conversation, George said, "Peter, I understand you are having a bit of a challenge with your mortgage due to getting laid off. Wanda and I talked about it, and we want to help you out with two or three months' worth of mortgage payments."

Not knowing what to say, Peter fumbled with his words before responding, "Hey, I appreciate the offer, but we can't take it."

"Why not?" George asked him.

"First, because I don't know when I might be able to pay you back. Second, my unemployment checks should begin before long, and that should tide us over."

"Who said anything about paying it back?" George asked. "This isn't a loan; it's a gift."

Peter still insisted he couldn't take it. Somehow he thought it would make him feel inadequate—a failure at supporting his family. In Peter's mind, if George had offered him a position at his company, or some means by which he could work off his debt, he could take the money without being made to feel small. Instead, he said in a stern tone of voice, "George, I appreciate the offer, but we can't take it." Then he hung up the phone, angry with his wife for telling someone of their troubles.

Peter's problem was pride. Instead of allowing a brother to minister to him, relying on the men with whom he was walking in a committed relationship, he tried to hide behind his mask. What Peter forgot is that we all face tough times in our lives, experience financial downturns, and struggle with our family or our faith. But with a brother beside you, you've got someone to help you through it.

When I feared for my life, I took strength in the fact that my brothers were close by me. I could have allowed pride to rule my life by later rationalizing that it was no big deal. But the truth is, had we been forced to turn and fight in the face of that danger, my chance of survival would have been greater because we were together.

Therefore, watch out for your pride. Learn to rely on your brothers. You need them, and they need you. A brother's commitment can help you through a tough time.

11
Walking Together

Bartering, which is a fair exchange of things of equal value, is beneficial but not bonding. Too often men treat each other like business colleagues, bartering for services but not ministering out of love. That's fine in the marketplace, but not in the family. God created us to bond—to blossom and become exporters of His grace and mercy. He expects us to treat each other like loving brothers, not as associates or competitors.

Jesus said that our oneness, our mutual concern and care, will show the world that the Father sent the Son. People *see God* through our loving actions. Not only that, it attracts them to Him. Unfortunately, our competitive culture has deluded some men into thinking they can make it on their own. We honor the Lone Ranger—the guy who works by himself, succeeding without the assistance of others. He believes he pulled himself up by his own bootstraps. That's a shame, because nobody makes it on his own.

Take a look at any business success, and you'll find a man dependent on other people. The self-made million-aire might have had a great idea, and he might have worked long hours to get to the top, but I'll guarantee you he didn't do it all by himself. Somebody worked with him. Somebody worked for him. Now that he's on top, somebody is managing things for him, or putting the pieces together, or filling out the paperwork, or tinkering with the machinery. A business is an organism as much as it is an organization.

Churches work the same way. We tend to think of a large, successful church as the result of the pastor's vision and hard work, but any pastor will tell you he couldn't do it without dedicated office help, competent support staff, and a committed band of praying saints. The Lord didn't come to earth to train individuals—He came to build a kingdom.

As men we have a tendency not to think of ourselves as "needy," but the fact is all of us have needs. Some need hope. Others need encouragement. Some need money. Others need to feel they are contributing to something important. But there is no greater value than true friendship. Is the reward of pursuing it worth the risk? You bet it is. Do not allow pride, selfishness, or a bad experience to run you away from friendship. Ministering to one another's needs binds you together like brothers in a family.

The Reward and the Risk

After I had spent a few years submitting to the Holy Spirit's work in my life through fellowshiping with other brothers, Gene, who had originally nurtured the tiny seedling planted in my heart, was the one person I needed to ask the question, "How do you define 'walking together'?" I thought about the men who had become close—Charles, Carl, my older brother James, and a couple of friends who had joined us—and I realized I couldn't explain it. Try as I might, I could not clearly articulate what it meant for brothers to walk together in committed relationships. So I contacted Gene.

For Gene, the process of "walking together" had been a slow and painstaking experience. After years of growing in relationships with various individuals, he told me that he had finally reached a conclusion: "You *can't* define it. You can't teach people how to 'walk together in committed relationships.' Somehow through our faithfulness to God and trust in His leadership, it just happens. The mask comes off, and you decide to follow Jesus together, mate."

As he continued to explain what he meant by that, in the middle of this eloquent exposition about God's mysterious ways of molding men, he stopped abruptly and said, "Well, Frank, we really cannot discuss this subject without talking to John." So with me still on the line in California, Gene phoned John in Maryland, and put us on a three-way hookup.

John Staggers was known to many people as Mr. Reconciliation. As he traveled across the nation and the world, he had an unusual ability to get people to sit down at the negotiating table and find solutions to problems in their lives and communities. John made several trips to South Africa, engaging leaders from all racial, tribal, and social groups in prayer and planning for equality and justice. He walked with mayors and presidents, and he never stopped being John.

During the urban unrest of the late sixties, when communities across America were being changed from places where people raised their families to a wasteland of charred buildings and businesses, John mobilized ex-convicts to stop the rioters. He played a pivotal role in preventing a large portion of the city of Washington, DC, from being burned to the ground.

With Gene, he had spent more than ten years seeking the ideal way to walk together as brothers in Christ. While their busy schedules slowly eroded the consistency of daily communication, the impact of their relationship upon both men's lives was profound.

After Gene and I greeted John and began tossing around in the playground of our imagination a memory full of fond times, something seemed different about John—Gene and I noticed a somber, uneasy silence across the telephone wires. The quiet was broken by the sound of a deep sigh from a normally effusive, exuberant man. As we asked him what was on his heart, John said he was tired. He had experienced deep hurt and disappointment after a lifetime of ministering to the broken, bruised, and neglected in our society. "At the very moment you brothers called," he said, "I was just telling God how tired I am. I'm tired of all the phoniness and the hypocrites."

I didn't know quite what to say, so I prayed. But Gene, always sensitive to the leading of the Spirit, began to talk about John as though he were not a part of the conversation. First he told me how he had met John, and the lost condition of his own soul. Then he went on to describe how his life had changed through their friendship. "When I met John," Gene continued, "I met Christ. Through his giving spirit and not-afraid-to-be-human attitude, I felt I'd finally seen God at work. There is no one on earth who made an impact on my life the way John did."

As Gene continued to share how his accomplishments in life, both spiritually and materially, had been inspired by John's example, I could hear John on the phone sobbing softly, yet profusely. Gene went on to detail one ministry after another that John had performed, and how the world was different because of his love. Finally, John pulled himself together and said, "You brothers will never, ever know what this phone call has meant to me."

A few scant years later, John Staggers passed away. At the celebration of his life, with people from throughout the nations lining the walls of the historic Third Street Church of God, Lt. Col. Oliver North, who had been assigned to a period of community service under John's supervision, recounted the tremendous impact John had had on his life. At the close of his remarks, clearly moved, he told how John had walked with him and become his friend while much of the world vilified him. One of the greatest things John taught him was still etched firmly in his mind. *"I wouldn't go across the street for a program, but I would go around the world for a relationship."*

Not a Program but a Process

The Lord didn't give us a *program* that every church is supposed to copy. He gave us a *process* which we're supposed to follow. So while there might not be an exact model we're all supposed to mimic, there are certainly principles we glean from the Gospels that reveal how Jesus walked with other men. Most of the things we learned from our men's fellowship group came from looking to the life of the Lord—like the importance of knowing Scripture, and spending time together, and seeking out ways to minister to one another and others.

The men involved attend different churches, in different denominations. We're not a program, but simply a group of men who have decided we can best grow in Christ if we commit to growing together.

The Priority of Relationships

A few years ago, several of us were invited to visit a church in South Carolina sponsoring a popular patriotic Christian musical. It starred members of the choir and some friends taking a leave of absence from Broadway, so it was a huge production. One guy, Todd, a small, bright, occasionally pushy fellow who owned a state-of-the-art recording studio, came along to see what it was like.

As a new believer, Todd was hungry for the Word, and I felt led to spend time with him, participate in helping disciple him and share the foundation of God's plan for his life. Todd and I represented two different generations in terms of age, and we were of different races, but the Bible says that God is no respecter of persons, and I felt the Lord leading me to take Todd under my wing.

Because of his family, he had spent his entire life around Hollywood personalities, but when he met Jesus, the Lord swept in and completely captured his heart. In Todd I saw no guile, just a deep determination to give God glory. His ordinary response to a problem that needed a solution was, "Yes, we can do it." I like being around that kind of individual, and we found ourselves praying, discussing the Scriptures, and talking about the challenges of marriage nearly every day. When we arrived at the theater where the scheduled rehearsals were in progress, we found the building beautiful but the sound horrendous. It was breaking up, cutting in and out, and bouncing all around the walls. Almost everyone was more than a little bit nervous, but Todd said, "We can fix this."

He showed up early the next morning just after dawn, worked nonstop throughout the entire day, and completely rewired the sound in that building. When the curtains went up for the first act, the audio was perfect. After the show, several members of the production came up to thank Todd for his wonderful gift, but he didn't see what the big deal was.

"They had a need for a sound man, and the Lord put me in the theater. What else could I do?" he asked me.

One never knows what gifts the Lord has invested in the individuals called to walk with you, but imagine the loss if the rest of us had refused to take the time to invest in Todd. Not only would his spiritual growth have suffered, but that show would not have been the same. We need each other. Even the crowds of people in the audience needed Todd, though they had no idea it was he who had made the production work. As we learn to take off the masks and walk with each other, the Spirit of God helps us begin to use our gifts to minister to those around us.

When you love Christ, you want to meet His family. Each member is unique, each with his own needs and his own gifts. It's easy to overlook those needs, or consider them an interruption. It's also easy to ignore your gifts or refuse to put them to use. There is risk in serving others—they might not appreciate it, or they might even reject your offer of help due to their pride. But the reward is a close-knit family of believers, who care for one another and look out for the needs of each other.

I'm a musician, and one of the things I've learned from my music is that *you never achieve harmony playing by yourself.* Harmony is only achieved when a number of people, each using their own gift to play their particular instrument, work together. When we do that, we create a beautiful and rich symphony to the glory of God.

12
Help When You Need It

Have you noticed how often you can get help when you don't need it? People are quick to give you advice when you don't need it. Banks want to lend you money when you don't need it. When you are on top, friends you haven't seen in months start to come around, flattering you and lavishing praise upon you. But when times get hard, those fair-weather friends have a tendency to disappear.

I remember a time in the early eighties when Bunny and I were going through an extremely tough season financially. We could not pay all of our monthly bills, nor did we envision in the foreseeable future a time when we would be able to catch up. My brothers and I would share information and pray on occasion about each one's challenges in general, but I did not mention needing any specific help. The need in my life required a miracle. Things got awfully tight for a while—it was very scary.

Then one Thursday morning, as I was sitting next to my friend Philip for a wonderful hour and a half of study and prayer, I discovered when I got home he had slipped a sizable check into the outside pocket of my trench coat. It was placed there just when we needed it most.

The next month, from out of the blue, we received a check in the mail from Gene for the exact amount necessary to make up the difference between what I had earned and what our monthly financial obligations were. I called Gene and thanked him, but he just laughed loudly and brushed it off saying, "It was nothing, mate."

Every month for the next six months, though we did not talk about it, Bunny and I received a check from Gene for the same amount. Then, unexpectedly, I received a telephone call from a film company located in New York, who requested permission to use one of the least-likely and less-productive songs from my music publishing catalog. After two months of negotiations, my attorney finalized the deal. We ended up with a huge advance and a sub-publishing agreement which yielded surplus funds. Long before I had an opportunity to inform Gene about this turn of events, I thought back and noticed that the checks from him had stopped coming at precisely the same time I received the call from the film company! As suddenly as they had begun, they stopped, as though they were controlled by a spigot turned on and off by the Lord.

However, God's blessings to us are never cut off. His only requirement is that we pass them on to others. "Freely you have received," it says in Matthew 10:8, "freely give."

Coincidence or Divine Design?

Now you might be thinking, "That was simply a coincidence. He happened to be there just when you needed him." That may be true, but suppose you had someone near you when you needed them. It doesn't take long to start believing that they are put there by God's design. They are there to help you escape a poor decision, a half hearted performance, or a personal dilemma. We may think we don't need anyone to try and help us, but the truth is we often need someone to warn us, stand nearby to steady us when we stumble, or help catch us if we fall.

I believe God has given to you the people you need. Often the brothers and sisters around you are the very persons God will use to help you when you need it. In the same way that flowers need sunshine and water to exist, people need people to help them survive and thrive in this lost world. You can either chalk up your brother's help to mere coincidence, or you can praise God for His divine design. He realizes that there are times when we simply need one another.

Has the battery in your car ever run down and all you needed was a quick boost to get going again? I have. Likewise, during those times in my life when I feel emotionally and physically run down, it is good to know I have someone close to encourage and spark me, so that I draw strength from the deep fountain of my own faith.

The Rock Church

In December of 1984, six months after our first trip to Africa, several of us went to Ethiopia to survey the ongoing effects of the famine in the mountainous, remote regions of that country. In order to reach the area, we had to travel on a military jet accompanied by heavily armed communist soldiers. It was a strange and tense flight.

Upon arriving in the northern province, we unpacked, ate a light dinner, and settled in for the night at a bombed-out enclave with no roof or toilet. We slept on a clean, cool, and hard concrete floor. Early the following morning, we were awakened by the constant drone of moans, interrupted by sounds of sharp, shrill wailing. I was deeply disturbed by this unknown and indecipherable sound, and was beginning to wonder if our decision to come to Ethiopia in the middle of a civil war and a famine was a bit crazy.

However, following an inquiry, I was informed by one of the relief workers that what we were hearing had become for them a familiar sound. Cutting through the cold dawn air each morning, it was the language of pain generated by the grief-stricken mothers losing so many of their children. They were joined by the elderly worshipers gathered at the front entrance to the Rock Church situated at the top of the mountain.

I told my traveling companion Glandion, who was standing nearby and who had overheard the conversation, "I'm going to go and see what it is all about." His reply was, "Let's walk together." Glandion Carney and I, along with several others, had all traveled to northern Ethiopia together, and were visiting for the same purpose—to see firsthand how we Americans could help our brothers. This morning we were all equally interested in a trip to the Rock Church, but were uncertain about the dangers of going alone. For obvious reasons, *walking together* made a lot of sense.

The location of the Rock Church was at the top of a steep incline. To get there required commitment. Once we arrived at the sight, we noticed all of the people—family members, friends, strangers—outside marching around the sanctuary. They were holding large rocks on their shoulders, while wailing out to God asking mercy for the people who were perishing. I asked one of them what it meant, and was told, "We are carrying stones of burden."

The circumstances of life had thrown these people together. They all had a common enemy, a common destiny, and a common community. To be a family entails more than sharing the same name—it requires commitment and a genuine concern for someone other than yourself. I saw that in those people. Although I could not directly feel their pain, I identified with their hurt. I was tempted to place a heavy stone upon my own shoulder for a while, and demonstrate with them my passion for their predicament.

The Scriptures suggest that ought to be the consistent attitude of anyone who has buried within his heart the seed of Christ's Spirit. We are to care for one another in brotherly love, thinking about those who need help because they have slipped and fallen. None of us is beyond temptation or so strong that the arrows of testing cannot penetrate our souls. Trials and tribulations are an equal opportunity employer—those we help now may not be the same ones called upon to help pull us through later. But what goes around comes around, and "whatsoever a man sows, *that* shall he also reap."

The Barometer of Relationships

Remember that time someone ran into the intersection of your life at precisely the right instance and saved you from a tragic mistake? Did you believe God sent them to help you? Did it ever occur to you the Lord may have arranged for you to meet them for more than a quick reminder of His love for you? Maybe God intends for you to actually get acquainted.

Of course, the problem is that sometimes you are called to love a brother or sister you don't really like. I once heard someone say, "To love the world is an easy chore. My problem is the guy next door." You see, that is because you can't run away from your neighbor. He's too close. Yet he isn't there by accident—God put him next to you as part of His purpose for your life.

It is possible that your most valuable relationship, inside or outside of your immediate family, is someone with whom you believe yourself to be incompatible. Yet imagine what the results might be if you and he made a conscious decision to walk together. The love of God would be even more evident. The world around you would see the grace and mercy of the Lord on display.

In His household, God is building a family filled with love, submitted to His laws, and unwavering in commitment to one another. The more we demonstrate our membership in that family, the more our lives bring glory to God. In many ways our relationships with others reveal the truth of our relationship with the Lord. We need one another to be human barometers of where we are in God.

And best of all, you and I are the benefactors. We are the ones who will reap the benefits of God's built-in harvest of enriched relationships tomorrow because of the seeds of brotherly affection we are planting into the soil of a friend today.

13
Investing in Men

Two years before I began the Thursday morning men's fellowship, Bunny and I organized the "Frank Wilson Bible Study Retreat." It was held twice a year at Arrowhead Springs, a beautiful foothill setting in southern California. The retreat's purpose was very simple: get away to relax and spend some isolated quality time with a few of our close friends. Along with them, we also invited those who were attending our weekly home Bible study, their families, and their friends.

Starting Friday evening, we would serve up an exciting dish of music and drama followed by a featured speaker. Then we would have a brief period of fellowship and prayer to conclude our program. Following breakfast the next morning, we would canvas the room looking for first-timers. We wanted to know their names, city of origin, why they decided to come, and who invited them. By the third year our little retreat had grown into a conference, its name changed to Dayspring, and we could usually expect to grow by about 50 to 60 new people every six months.

Ripe for Recruitment

On one particular morning, after approximately 15 persons had shared their stories, a tall, brown-skinned man dressed in business attire cracked the crisp but jubilant air, exhibiting a commanding presence and a huge, deep booming voice.

"Good morning," he began. "My name is Don Dudley. I am from the Pacific Northwest—Seattle, Washington—and I am here out of curiosity."

With his big voice and bigger presence, Don got everybody's attention. "A good friend of mine, Barbara Williams, phoned me the other day and said that she was on her way to the West Coast. She invited me to join her. When I asked her why she was coming, she responded, 'To spend a few days walking with a brother.' So that's why I'm here. I am curious to find out what she meant by the phrase 'walking with a brother.' Especially if you know Barbara."

Laughter cascaded around the room. Barbara Williams was an extremely attractive, articulate, and confident woman. I met her through a couple who had been discipling her. If you were to meet Barbara today, you would find her to be an extraordinarily gifted speaker and Bible teacher. She eventually became the wife of Tom Skinner, one of the foremost evangelists of our day and president of the organization he founded.

I had only met Barbara over the phone until she decided to attend one of our conferences. The conference itself proved to be incidental to the friendship. She was an excellent student, a quick learner who excelled in grasping the language and lessons of the Word of God. Still, when I first met Barbara, I discovered she trusted almost no one. She had a hard shell on, though she was a genuinely caring individual who worked endless hours assisting the plight of poor people both nationally and internationally. She served as executive director of the Congressional Black Caucus, and was much in demand as a speaker. When it came to her spiritual life, however, she was dry. A lot of crud had latched onto her heart and calcified it. A bad childhood and betrayals by supposedly close friends had stolen away her confidence in people. In short, this was a woman ripe for recruitment to a friendship in Christ.

That's what the family brought to Barbara. She found brothers and sisters with whom she could walk. She found people facing the same struggles, dealing with the same sin issues, and trying to live down the same problems from the past. But her life was changing when she came to Dayspring—and in her participation she found fellow believers willing to trust her and walk with her. Slowly her shell came off, and she soon found herself walking in a community with other believers. In turn, Barbara began telling others about the changes in her life, and that led to her invitation for Don to join us.

Time for Investment

What you quickly discover about people like Barbara is that many of their associates are also spiritually dry. Such was the case with Don. He was the head of the Board of Human Resources for a major city and a successful owner of a popular radio station. But inside of Don lay a potter's graveyard. He had been separated from his wife, Carol, for over a year, estranged from his children, and was becoming deeply embroiled in a nasty political battle.

Following that morning's message, Don responded to the invitation, crying unashamedly and acknowledging his need for the Lord. He desperately wanted to find the peace and joy that comes from knowing Jesus Christ, and he needed a brother to walk with him in that new life.

Because Don was such a dear friend to Barbara, and so desperately hungry for spiritual food, I decided to invest some time into his life, getting to know him and his family. Occasionally I would call and talk with him about the wonders of God's love, reminding him of the endlessness of the Lord's divine grace. Don soaked up these spiritual truths like a desert that had never known moisture. He longed for God's grace in his life.

Six months would pass before the next Dayspring conference was scheduled. Almost as soon as announcements were mailed out, Don was on the phone saying he wanted to bring his wife, from whom he was separated. Carol was a beauty queen, extremely intelligent and talented. She was an excellent pianist and flutist, but inside her soul she was parched—brittle, bleached, and precariously fragile. At that conference, Carol accepted Christ, and their relationship was reconciled. Although Don and Carol's marriage remained rocky at times, it was wonderful to watch their spiritually darkened countenances become gradually transformed into beacons of light.

Sometime later, I got a phone call. It was Don, and he was ecstatic. Carol was going to be baptized that following Saturday morning at a church in Seattle where they had become members. He made it sound as though she was about to receive the Nobel prize, the Pulitzer, and an Oscar combined. I got so caught up in his state of euphoria that I purchased a plane ticket and flew up to witness the baptism and encourage the two of them in their newfound faith. All that couple needed was some encouragement to replenish their spiritual life and a brother to walk with them through the hard times.

A few months went by and it was time for another Dayspring. This time Don showed up with his mom and dad, his wife's sister and brother-in-law, as well as one of his children from a previous marriage. Each one of those people decided to entrust their lives to the Lord on that weekend. A little investment on the part of a brother paid eternal dividends in that family.

Brothers

I once heard it said that people don't care how much you know until they know how much you care. I suppose that sums up the tremendous impact my visit for Carol's baptism had on Don's life. What we had attempted to teach him over many hours of fellowship on the telephone—what it means to be a brother—he understood in one moment of friendship. *A friend is a friend when he acts like one. And brothers stick together.*

Don later revealed how he was caught completely off guard by my actions, disarming his natural suspicions and concerns. At first he didn't quite know what to make of my interest in his life. But as the weeks rolled by, that became less of a consideration. Spending time in the Word of God with some of the brothers led him to realize we cared about him. The investment of time changed his life.

Whenever Don's schedule brought him to Los Angeles, he would make it a point to spend the night at our home and travel with me to the Thursday morning men's fellowship. He had a sharp and disciplined mind, and he was growing rapidly in biblical knowledge and spiritual zeal.

Your Investment Portfolio

During the next two years, Don was consumed with developing his understanding of the new creation he had become in the Lord Jesus. He was determined to know how his life in Christ could be integrated into his professional life. One day he phoned me and said, "Frank, I believe I am being called into full-time Christian ministry."

I quickly challenged him with, "Don, have you thought about the possibility that perhaps you are being called to pray more, have a deeper walk, a more sanctified lifestyle, or simply to become more involved in the local church where you are a member?"

But Don insisted. "I've prayed about it, Frank, and I'm certain. The Lord wants me as His servant."

I reluctantly said, "All right," then asked him, "So what's next?" He indicated his intent to find a seminary where he could receive formal training while remaining close to his family and his local support network. Then we prayed together as he began the process of searching for a school and employment on the West Coast. It was to no avail. After a few months of frustrating failure, Don received an unbelievably attractive solicitation from the head of Volunteers of America. He was offered the position as their national public relations director, and saw it as the Lord's opportunity to minister. Feeling beside himself with joy, Don could barely speak as he called to tell me the news. He immediately began making plans to take up his new position at Volunteers of America headquarters in the city of New Orleans.

The Lord had worked out all the details, for this was the city in which Carol had grown up and spent most of her life. Her mom, dad, and two of her sisters were still living there. On top of that, Don received a letter inviting him to attend Baptist Theological Seminary located in New Orleans. When he called to tell me, we began talking about the changes apparent in his life. A few short years earlier, Don had been angry, confused, and separated from everyone close to him. His marriage was on the rocks, his children were estranged, and he had been far from God. The only thing that could be called a "success" in his life was his career, but that had only served to increase his frustration. What man wants a great career without someone with whom he can share it?

Now everything was changed. His marriage was back together. He had a close relationship with his kids. He was in the center of God's will, using his gifts and abilities to serve the Lord. More than that, he had peace with God and a clear sense of purpose in his life. The fact that a few brothers had been willing to invest in his life had made an eternal difference.

"If it hadn't been for your investment," he told me over the phone, "my life would never have turned around." The men's fellowship group had helped him take off his mask, discover how to open up, learn to love others, and find a new relationship with God. I have often heard Carl Martin, a brother in our fellowship say, "Walking together in accountable relationships not only contributes to growth, but *reveals* growth. It lets you know where you are in your walk with God." Investing in the lives of men is costly, but it pays huge dividends.

14
Respect for Accountability

A pastor I know arrived in Houston International Airport on a Friday evening and checked into a nearby hotel due to an overnight layover. He was traveling to a large city on the southernmost tip of South America, and a flight out of Houston early Saturday morning was the only one that could assure his timely arrival to a very important meeting.

Sharing the elevator with him as he traveled up to his hotel suite was an appetizingly beautiful and vivacious young woman with reddish-brown hair and hazel eyes. She was conservatively dressed, with a carefully crafted structure—what my buddies would refer to as "drop-dead gorgeous." They began a brief conversation, exchanging names and mere small talk about where they were from and where they were going as they continued up the elevator to their rooms. Coincidentally, after shaking hands good night, they both exited on the same floor. He looked admiringly at the young lady as she passed by in what seemed like slow motion, and she noticed him fidgeting with his key before placing it into the lock and entering his room for the evening.

Approximately 45 minutes elapsed before, while watching the national news on television, he heard a soft knock on his door. Looking through the peephole, he caught a big surprise. Standing in his doorway was this same lovely creature wearing a light travel coat over a sheer nightgown. He didn't know whether to respond or pretend to have turned in for the evening. His curiosity, however, got the best of him, so he opened the door and asked while swallowing hard, "Hello . . . what can I do for you?"

Hesitant at first, she nervously turned her head, looking first one way and then the other down both directions of the corridor, until turning to face him again and saying, "I'm . . . just a little bit lonely. I couldn't sleep, and was wondering if you might not want some company for the evening?"

Before he answered, my friend rehearsed his thoughts. Then he took a deep breath and said, "Joan, there are at least four reasons why I cannot risk inviting you into my room. One, you are very attractive, and I would probably have no trouble at all being seduced by a person as desirable as you. Two, I am already married, and I made a vow to my wife when I got married that I'd always be faithful to her. Three, I also made a promise to a close group of friends, and I cannot let my covenant brothers down. They are counting on me to stay strong for the sake of our mutual agreement to resist this sort of temptation. And last but not least, I must avoid any path which may lead to my becoming an embarrassment to the name of Christ."

The young lady stood there looking both stunned and puzzled, so he suggested they meet in the coffee shop and he would explain to her what all of that meant. Due to the stress of his busy schedule, the needs of his church, and the constant irritation caused by his children's rebelliousness, that man's relationships were under a great deal of strain. Not surprisingly, he was tempted. Who wouldn't be? For several years, that pastor had been struggling in his marriage. His sex life was in the doldrums, he had needs that were being left unfulfilled, and the stress of his schedule cried out for some sort of release.

At the same time, that pastor thought about all the times he had encouraged his own men, from the pulpit and in person, to resist this same temptation. Rather than reasoning that he "deserved" to sin, he decided to honor the covenant of Christ above his feelings. In a sense, that man was sticking his finger in the dike, holding back a flood of disastrous consequences for his marriage and family.

He hurriedly dressed, all the while praying for wisdom. When he arrived on the first floor, she was waiting, though now fully dressed. After sitting down in the restaurant, she immediately began inquiring as to his thinking. "Though I may not understand it, I respect the wife thing, and the religious side of things as well. But I have seen many married men, and even some members of the clergy, who had absolutely no problem making it with one of my girlfriends. Please don't misunderstand me— this is not something I am in the habit of doing. It's just that when I looked into your warm eyes, and felt the strength of your tender touch as we shook hands on the elevator, at that moment I knew you were the perfect man for me. I wanted to be with you if only for one night."

He took a minute before responding to her words, admitting, "I know that what you are saying about others is true. But I share a commitment with a few brothers that, for the rest of our time on earth, we would hold each other accountable in seeking first the kingdom of God in all areas of our lives. It could be that the only reason we did so is because God knew the day would come when I would meet you at this hotel and have an opportunity to tell you about His love, peace, and the awesome price He paid for our salvation."

Then, slowly and lovingly, he led that young woman into a saving knowledge of Jesus Christ. Today she heads a national ministry, touching lives all across America.

Fantasy Island

The truth is, far too many men today don't hold to their commitments. Their attitude is, "I don't want to get caught and suffer the consequences, but if I can get away with it, I will." On business trips, or while away from their wives and families, they conduct completely different lives. Unfortunately, men who exist that way must always wear a mask.

When they are at home, they wear the mask of a family man. When they are away from home, they slip into a different role. Being unsure of themselves and their values, they find themselves living in a world of make-believe, where sin has no consequences and actions don't shape character. On the outside they go through the motions of asserting superiority and insisting upon respect. But on the inside, they are insecure men with no respect for themselves.

Not being happy with who they have become and not knowing who they are drives them into the arms of fantasy.

A man who wants desperately to be viewed as a lady's man will act out his fantasies whenever he can. He acts like the leader in his home, usually without ever being taught what that means, but he gets stuck when his situation demands he lead where he has not gone himself. It's almost impossible for him to admit when he's wrong. He has to always be right. He has difficulty acknowledging pain, even when the hurt is indescribable, and every loss for him is a lethal blow against his manhood. Unable to bend, he breaks. Unable to cry, he cracks. This kind of man does not realize that momentary failure is but a stepping-stone to lasting success. Instead, he becomes a pawn of his pursuits. Through careful management of his emotional insecurities, his sinful behavior is never dealt with, only disguised. He goes through life respected for what he is not, never dealing with who he is, and not ever fully approaching his God-given potential.

My psychology friends would doubtless say that a man's ego learns to modify behavior by controlling impulses that are socially unacceptable, substituting appropriate actions when he deems it necessary. My sociology friends would argue that men are taught rules regarding how they should respond to their day-to-day circumstances. But my Bible shows me that a man who sins is a sinner.

Lucifer got kicked out of heaven and is bound for hell because he thought he was someone he is not. Cain thought by killing Abel he was elevating himself, but he was not. Jacob thought he was fooling everyone when he stole his brother's birthright, but he was not. A man who is unwilling to admit that he is lost may have a fool for a guide, and many of the things men do to seek attention lead to emptiness because what they really want is respect.

If you want respect, you must live with respect for others.

In Pursuit of Respect

Reggie Williams was one of the top linebackers in the National Football League a few years ago. At the time, his drive to play was not the money, but the respect of pro sports. His mental frame toward the opposing player was simple: "If you're coming, bring your best shot." Reggie communicated a certain cavalier kind of cockiness. To the women, he was an attractive playboy looking for a mate. To the men, he was a tough guy looking for a fight. But those who really understood him and could see beneath the thin veneer of self-assurance and bravado knew that he was a man searching for meaning. A number of forces were weighing upon him: debts over cars and clothes, pressures with women, materialism and all of its trappings. On top of all of that, he was a man void of spirituality.

One day, his right knee collapsed. It was Reggie's first serious sports injury, and it was devastating. Depressed, he thought he would have to leave the game. But he was sent to Los Angeles, to one of the foremost sports doctors in the world, Dr. Frank Jobe, for surgery. When he arrived in Los Angeles, he was carrying a freight train full of baggage, afraid for his future and seeking direction in his life. Terri McFaddin, a close friend of mine and popular songwriter, met him and introduced him to the men's fellowship.

Since Reggie had decided to stay around Los Angeles long enough to test the results of his surgery, we began to walk with him. He was invited by the brothers to church, and to Dayspring, and slowly his fears and anxieties gave way to faith. More than six months passed before Reggie returned home for rehabilitation and a chance at a comeback with the Cincinnati Bengals. He overcame the injury and raised the level of his play to a new high, eventually becoming an all-pro in the NFL.

Before he left LA, I asked him what he thought about when his knee gave out. He told me, "It's funny, but I thought about a Scripture I had heard once during chapel service while I was still a student at Dartmouth College. It read, 'At the name of Jesus, every knee shall bow, and every tongue confess that Jesus Christ is Lord.' I thought about my knee bowing, and wondered if this was God's answer to my arrogance."

Reggie told me he had spent his life in pursuit of respect on the playing field. Instead, he was humbled by his situation. It wasn't until he got into an accountability relationship with some brothers that he was able to see that his empty pursuit was the result of not recognizing who he was in Jesus Christ. When he got right with God, his need to portray himself as a tough guy faded. He was still a great ball player, but now he could afford to be vulnerable and allow others to get close to him. He not only became a better football player, he became a better man.

Fellowship Without Accountability

The situations in life which inspire within us the greatest amount of self-doubt are often the very things God will use to enhance our acquisition of faith. And if you've got a friend to help you through the hard times and hold you accountable for your actions, you'll find yourself a stronger person. So ask yourself, "Do I have a brother to whom I am submitted?" If your wife was distressed about your marriage and felt you were not being responsive to her attempts to discuss it with you, could she call your brother without hurting your ego? Do you pretend to be accountable, when really you are hiding everything that's hurting you?

My brothers need to know how I'm really doing, not just how I'm looking. As my buddy Carl Martin often says, *"Fellowship without accountability is of limited benefit."* A man doesn't just need friends—he can get those anywhere. The local tavern is filled with guys who want to hang out, to find someone with whom they can commiserate, or to see if they can get something from you. But a Christian man needs brothers—those who will find the real you, check with you when you need it, and hold you accountable to do the right thing. Those are also the types who will stick with you, even when you blow it.

My friend Rock was a brilliant businessman with great leadership qualities. But Rock had a hidden problem: His wife seemed to be in complete charge at home. She even disrespected him in public. He appeared to pass those situations off, but inside Rock was seething with anger. On the outside, he was a picture of strength and stability. But on the inside, his life was in serious decay. He developed a cocaine problem, and his life started spinning out of control. That's when a brother, who was part of the Thursday morning fellowship and who ran a drug treatment facility, stepped in to help. He was willing to take Rock on as a personal project. You see, you don't throw away your family—you throw them a rope when they are falling, or a raft when they are drowning. Rock is in recovery today, even though the struggle has been costly to his family and his health.

When I asked him why he'd become involved with drugs, he told me it was his anger. He'd feel so much anger inside that it drove him to destructive behaviors. It nearly destroyed his life, but today Rock is alive, teaching Bible studies, and he no longer wears a mask. He has seen others respect and love him, and he has been set free from his old way of thinking.

When you know you are loved just the way you are, it makes you free to be yourself with other people. Rock told me he felt like he always had to be Moses—the group leader, the one everyone looked to, even though he knew his marriage and personal life was in shambles. But in wearing that mask, he became like Moses in another way, veiling his face so that others couldn't see the glory of God fading from his life.

That's a choice every man has. He can stay where he is, in his present condition, pretending to have it all together, or he can become accountable to his brothers and be transformed.

To obey God is better than putting on our Sunday morning religious false-face and pretending. Accountability in relationships encourages obedience to God's word. As a consequence of our obedience, we grow and experience more of His glory. The visible manifestations of His attributes and character begin to show up in our lives.

15
Like Dry Bones

Accountability among men can not only encourage obedience, but it can also renew a man spiritually. One morning during the early days of our group, the lead singer for one of the world's most popular rock bands walked into our fellowship with his mask off. After sitting down, without any consideration for where we were in our discussion, he confessed, "I've got a date tonight, fellows. Talk me out of it!"

Initially, everyone was stunned speechless. Some thought it was a joke, but Philip wasn't laughing. He began to relate how he had been feeling about his life, his marriage, and struggles in his relationship with God.

He had been married to Janet for almost ten years. They had two beautiful children, and another on the way. They had success, money, and prestige in the industry. But their marriage had been empty and "convenient." It had been years, it seemed, since they were connected emotionally, spiritually, or socially. So we began to talk about Phil's life and his walk with God. We did talk him out of his date, but in the midst of our conversation it became clear that Phil's soul was dry. It needed nourishment from some brothers who were holding him responsible for his actions, as they would want him to do on their behalf.

We reached out to help him. We spent time with him, canvasing the Scriptures together and nurturing his faith in God. What we saw in return was the strengthening of an anemic spiritual life. Slowly, as we open ourselves up to God's grace and encourage one another toward holy living, our spiritual dryness is replaced with a rich garden of delight in the Lord.

Walking in the Valley

Many people we know are languishing in the throes of a searing and life-depleting spiritual desert. In the book of Ezekiel it is written,

> The hand of the LORD was upon me, and carried me out in the spirit of the LORD, and set me down in the midst of the valley which was full of bones, and caused me to pass by them round about: and, behold, there were very many in the open valley; and, lo, they were very dry. And he said unto me, Son of man, can these bones live? And I answered, O Lord GOD, thou knowest. Again he said unto me, Prophesy upon these bones, and say unto them, O ye dry bones, hear the word of the LORD. Thus saith the Lord GOD unto these bones: Behold, I will cause breath to enter into you, and ye shall live (37:1-5 KJV).

Ezekiel knew about dry-bone experiences. He had seen firsthand what happens when people allow their spiritual conditions to shrivel: lifeless and bleached bones. The prophet of God was standing amidst a boneyard, with nothing but death and dryness surrounding him. And all it took to bring life to those old bones was the Word of God.

Have you ever felt your spiritual life was nothing but dry bones? That there was no life or freshness to your walk with God? If so, *don't blame God.* The Lord isn't the one who caused your spiritual life to slack off. If you feel far away from Him, it's because *you* moved. Each of us is responsible for his own walk. Neither should you blame your circumstances. God sometimes allows us to go through hard times for His own purposes, but they don't cause spiritual dryness. To the contrary, they draw us closer to His refreshing spring. *Your problems are not the instruments of your pain, they are messengers of God's grace.* God has chosen to allow you to go through them for His own purposes—perhaps so that you will be able to relate to the souls left stranded in the valley of dry bones.

You see, God wants our attention focused upon His priorities. You are surrounded by people who are searching for life-giving spiritual water. He has set each of us down in the midst of a valley of dry bones. For where men and women are lost, it is dry. Where babies are having babies and killing babies before they have them, it is dry. Where drugs and alcohol are popular choices for momentary psychological excursions, it is dry. Where marriages are folding fast and the nuclear family is quietly disappearing off the screen of the future, it is indeed dry. When a culture decides to turn its back on the truth of God in order to embrace the lies of Satan, it is very dry. And yet they have potential for becoming an exceedingly great army for God.

Even if people look defeated, half-dead, or buried in a boneyard, God still has the power to speak life, raise them, and stand them upon their feet. What He has instructed His people to do is to tell them the truth: "O ye dry bones, hear the word of the LORD." Those thirsty people need to hear a message from God like you have discovered, and they will find life!

Can Bones Live?

Unfortunately, I'm not sure if all Christians today have the vision or compassion to offer life. The Lord wants us to bring resurrection to dead people, discarded souls; but too often we are preoccupied with creating our own pleasurable kingdoms, and ignore the voice of God. Ask yourself: Do you believe these bones can live? The fornicator and adulterer, the thief, liar, and drunkard? Can God use you as part of His eternal plan to stand them upon their feet?

The Lord asked His prophet, "What do you see, Ezekiel?"

The answer came back: "Bones."

So the Lord asked, "What about them is readily noticeable?"

"They have no life," Ezekiel answered.

"Anything else?"

"They are dry."

So the Lord inquired, "What does that tell you?"

"They are dead. They have been for a long, long time."

Then the Lord asked Ezekiel the all-important question: "Can these bones live?"

That's a question we all ought to consider every day as we come into contact with people. Men and women from all walks of life display irrefutable evidence that they are spiritually dead. Some of them are people with whom you work. A few you see right in church. They want God and they need God, but they have settled for dead and lifeless religions.

Can these bones live? Brother, God is in the business of bringing life out of deadness. The question is not, Can He do it? but Will you be a part of His plan to do so? He wants to use you to uplift others, whether they are a stranger or a brother. It is done as you help another experience the love and mercy of God, explore the truths of

God's holy Word together, and apply those principles to your lives. Yours is refreshed and renewed in the process as you pray through difficult situations, believing in God to move, and watching Him touch lives. Even if those He touched were nothing but dry bones, the heart of the Lord still aches to see them standing in their rightful place.

16
Nails for the Carpenter

My father was sort of a jack-of-all-trades. It seemed like he could fix anything: televisions, radios, refrigerators, washing machines, most anything electrical, many of which were dead on arrival. Somehow my dad couldn't bring himself to bury the dead items. They just remained in a state of purgatory, occupying a corner of the garage.

Besides these odd jobs, he was also a builder. The first house we owned was one that he had built. I recall observing him before his early-morning starts—pulling out the toolbox, grabbing a bag full of used nails, and handling his hammer. As carpenters will sometimes tell you, very good nails are often used nails. They have been tested, and the substance out of which they are made has been revealed. Many of these old nails had been bent, possibly from a poorly placed blow or an attempted puncture of an unyielding obstacle. My dad would lay them on their sides and hammer them back into their original straight position, then he would pound them into place on the house.

Dad always seemed to know exactly how to hit the nail on the head. When he hit 'em, they performed as though they were perfect nails—like new, not bent at all. Occasionally my father would allow me to go along and watch him build, holding tools for him or picking up scraps of wood. My job description for a while was to pick up the used nails and let Dad the carpenter straighten, position, and place them into the frames and joints of the buildings. Every now and then I would ask if I could hammer a few nails for him. I hated the used, bent nails he gave me. Even after I had straightened one of them out, as soon as I would try and hit it, it would instantly rebend. The whole process was discouraging to me, and I probably destroyed more nails than I saved.

But I learned an important lesson from watching my dad: *Even bent nails can be put to use.* He would see me start to throw away a bent nail, and he would stop me with a sharp word: "What do you think you're doing? You don't throw away a perfectly good nail just because it's bent. Here, let me have it." Then he would patiently pick up the bent nail and start tapping on it, until he had worked out the kinks.

There is a close resemblance to many of our lives being like bent nails. The bends characterize mistakes. The flattened edges indicate our own unsuccessful attempts at rectifying situations. At one time, we were all like that— a bunch of bent nails, all needing to be straightened so that we could be used. I'll occasionally hear about a brother's ungodly behavior and wonder, "Why can't he get it right?" I may even try to help him, only to watch the guy make more of a mess out of his life. Instead of getting better, things get worse. In that sort of situation, it's easy to just avoid the guy. Reject him. Write him off. Because he ought to know better. I'll pray that God will take care of it all, then forget about it.

Master Carpenter

I'm glad God doesn't treat us that way. He is in the job of reclaiming bent nails, not throwing them away. The more time I spend watching the Lord touch lives and heal hurts, the more I believe that no life deserves to be thrown away. I learned from watching my dad not to waste materials, and I wonder at the grace of God for not wasting lives. He knows how to reconstruct and use them expertly, as they were intended, just as my father knew how to reclaim a bent nail. Even though my dad never obtained a high school education, he was a master carpenter. God is, in a much greater way, the same.

The Lord doesn't waste materials. He is the Master Carpenter. God looks beyond the disfigured coating of corrupt, decaying mankind, sights an image of promise, and concludes that He paid a huge cost to salvage each individual and make him a part of His family.

Thomas, who was not present when Jesus appeared to His disciples in the upper room, insisted, "Unless I can see in His hands the print of the nail, and put my finger into the print of the nails, I will not believe." His reluctance to believe without first seeing has earned him the title of "doubting Thomas," and maligned the memory of his unfailing faith and well-documented record of spreading the gospel throughout the first-century world. Thomas was a bent nail, but God used him in a mighty way.

Peter was a loud, brash fisherman who made promises he couldn't keep. At the Garden of Gethsemane he acted rashly, and a few hours after assuring the Lord of his undying devotion, he denied ever having met Jesus. Peter was a bent nail, whom most pastors would have given up on. But the Lord didn't give up—He saw the value in Peter's life. He will never forsake His followers. He will never throw them away.

The world is full of people who have not yet seen the resurrected Lord and who, due to their lack of faith, doubt His existence. But they believe when they see the love of Jesus in us, embracing the least and the lost. When they observe a demonstration of an uncommon commitment between those of us who proclaim ourselves to be His disciples, they believe.

God is not intimidated when we ask Him questions, nor is He angry when we are anxious about our uncertainties. He wants us to be sure of His commitment to us. "Thomas," He says to the doubter, "reach here your finger and behold my hand; and reach here your hand and place it in My side, and be not faithless, but believe." In other words, "Reach your finger into the nail hole. I'm still here with you." Jesus left none feeling like rejects, not even the deserters.

The Price

Three nails were necessary to fasten Jesus securely to the cross for His crucifixion. As two ripped savagely into His palms, pinning flesh and bones onto the surface of that tree, the other was driven mercilessly through His feet. His suffering was gruesome without measure.

What Satan and all of those who participated did not know is that those nails were implements of divine intent. They were crude and simple instruments used for securing in place the foundation for a holy habitation of God called the church. Perhaps had they known, they would have devised an alternative plot. When Christ died on that cross, He set free every sinner, every loser, and every bent nail.

After His death was made certain by the soldiers that dark and dismal Friday afternoon 2000 years ago, Christ's body was carefully removed from the cross. It was dressed and buried in a new tomb that belonged to a Pharisee and secret disciple named Joseph of Aramathea—a man who was too afraid to call himself a follower of Jesus while He walked the earth. My Bible tells me the Lord loved even bent, cowardly men enough to die for their sins. More than that, as He lay dying on that cross, Jesus asked His Father to forgive the very men putting Him to death. He was willing to give His life for men you and I would probably throw away. He is the God of restoration, willing to pay the price to straighten out the most worthless, bent nails in history.

Many of us in the church are like those nails. We have been used, bent, and shoved out of contention, lying around the scrap heap of this world's woes. When we began to wonder if our lives had become completely spent, someone arrived to pick us up and deliver us into the tool bag of the wise Carpenter. A nail is not able to straighten itself, and neither are we. Being straightened is our desire—we all want to be removed from the consumption of corrosion and placed into the arena of purposeful activities.

That happens when we are walking together. As we encourage and challenge each other, pray with one another and apply Scripture to life, we slowly see the kinks bent out, the imperfections exposed. As we realize the true nature of our condition and confess it, God understands and forgives our ignorance. Then He strengthens us while we submit to the painful process of change. The ones who are grateful will begin a life of helping other people recover rather than being tossed into the waste bin of used-up humanity.

Like the spikes used to crucify Him, Jesus finds a very similar implement useful for fixing the frame of His house. Though a storm rises, threatening to tear portions of the structure apart, situated between every joint, connecting the walls and rooms within the entire building, is a device He has designed, which pledges an unwavering attachment to each individual part. It's called love. And just like the nails, if love is to work it has to be used.

Down But Not Out

Mel Hanton was feeling victimized and rejected, dumped like a sack of bent nails. He had just been axed from a position at a well-known organization without an explanation, but suspected it was politically motivated.

With no means of support and nowhere to turn, and with vengeful thoughts racing around in his head unchecked, he shared his humiliating hurt with a close friend by the name of Gwen. She did not know quite what to say to him, but she knew about some men who met at 6:00 A.M. each Thursday morning for the express purpose of learning how to love another brother.

Therefore on the next day, she picked him up and brought him to the restaurant around 6:30 A.M. As they walked through the door, Gwen looked around before spotting the roped-off section where we were seated. Mel was clearly uneasy, knowing he was a stranger in the midst of several men he had never met. The expression on his face told a thousand tales, while the dimness in his eyes disclosed the damage resulting from his overnight bout with sleeplessness.

"Brothers," we were told, "this is Mel. He's a friend of mine. He has some issues, and I told him he needed to talk with you."

We pointed him to a seat, then returned to our dialogue regarding the meaning and application of some Bible passage. Since we had no particular agenda other than learning how to listen to God and develop a more sensitive spirit toward one another, we figured that morning was made for Mel.

Hearing men openly and honestly express what was going on in their lives must have been awfully reassuring for him, because when he was asked what was happening in his life, Mel quickly revealed the depths of his disappointment, disillusionment, and his feelings of being betrayed.

After a few moments, a question was then posed to him: "Mel, do you know the Lord?"

He paused before answering, "No, I guess not."

"Well, we've found that many times the problems experienced in our lives are nothing more than urgent telegrams from God, attempting to capture our attention before we run out of time. Could it be that God wants to get your attention?" Then we carefully explained God's love and the price He paid for our salvation. Slowly and prayerfully, the gospel was explained, and the question was asked, "Would you like for Christ to come into your life?"

Without hesitation, Mel replied, "Yes, I would." Then he humbly bowed his head in prayer and received the Lord.

We found out he was separated from his wife and children, and wanted to go home to see if he could restore his family. We learned he was from Dayton, Ohio, and asked one of the brothers to check and see what it would cost to send him home. A phone call was made, we received the information, and someone suggested, "Brothers, let's send him home." Everyone agreed—even those struggling financially themselves.

So Mel went home. His family was reunited. He subsequently decided that he needed to return to school and get his master's degree. We introduced him to several of the brothers on the East Coast. We all kept in touch with Mel from time to time.

Later, he decided to attend law school. He received his law degree and is now an attorney on the New York Stock Exchange. He loves the brothers, he loves his family, and he loves Jesus. People who knew Mel those many years ago wouldn't recognize him today. His life is filled with joy and laughter, and he purposefully seeks out those he can help.

Do you know what made the difference? Love. The Master Carpenter loved that bent nail too much to throw it away. His desire was to rescue it. God wants each one of us to become a useful instrument, a nail in a sure place, helping to build an ever-expanding house of praise to His glory. God recognizes a man who is down, but not out. He loves even the character who appears to all the world as a loser.

Paul, in describing the house of God, writes,

> Now you are no longer strangers to God and for-eigners to heaven, but you are members of God's very own family, citizens of God's country, and you belong in God's household with every other Christian. What a foundation you stand on now: the apostles and the prophets; and the cornerstone of the building is Jesus Christ himself! We who believe are carefully joined together with Christ as parts of a beautiful, constantly growing temple for God. And you also are joined with him and with each other by the Spirit, and are part of this dwelling place of God (Ephesians 2:19-22 TLB).

As brothers, we are called to build that house together—bent nails and all.

17

Where Is Your Brother?

Have you ever looked at an old photo-graph of people and wondered about the whereabouts of those pictured? It's natural to want to know who they are, what they were doing, and what's happened to them since the photo was taken. That happened to me not long ago. I was visiting the home of Jenny Jamison, a stout, compact woman in her early fifties. She has a slight reddish tinge to her hair, sprinkled with a bit of gray, but her face is young and adorned with designer-framed reading glasses and a ready smile.

Jenny is not a wealthy woman, but you can see she is rich in relationships from studying the pictures in her home. There are plenty of old, faded photographs framed upon the walls and upon small tables, as well as recent shots projecting the faces of family members and friends during their happiest times.

Jenny loves people. In fact, she loves to love people. It seems that those photographs are tributes to the people she has served and loved over the years. One day, as I stopped by for a brief meeting, I noticed that, while I rec-ognized most of the people in her pictures, there was one stranger on her walls.

"Jenny, who is this?" I asked, pointing at a smiling face.

"Oh, child," she replied, "that's my baby brother."

"And where is he?"

She stopped for a brief moment, looking off into space as though trying to catch a momentary glimpse of him passing. Then, continuing with a disappointed sigh, she replied, "I don't know. I hear from him every now and then, but he moves around a lot. I hear he's in Dallas or someplace near there. He's sort of a rollin' stone. Seems like everybody is so scattered."

"Yes," I said to her. "It's hard when you lose touch with those you love."

"That's what makes us family," Jenny said to me. "You don't choose family like you choose friends. You're there for family—mistakes and all."

Her remarks reminded me of my own friend Rob, who has two younger brothers he loves, but who has had to watch those boys struggle with staying out of trouble. No matter what, Rob has been there for them at every turn. Through their substance abuse, broken families, homelessness, and a combination of problems caused by poor decisions, Rob has stayed with his brothers. Ask him where they are, and he will probably drop his head, admit he doesn't know, yet tell you he loves them anyway.

In reality, they are not close. After all Rob has tried to do for them, those boys don't appreciate any of his efforts. But they're still brothers, so Rob still cares. As family, he can't help but care. His brothers may have problems, but Rob is always there to try and help them through the difficult times.

I guess every family has its share of problems—even the Lord had family troubles. When He came to His own people, they rejected Him outright. Nearly 2000 years ago, the apostle John recorded God's response to Israel's rejection: "He came into his own world, but his own nation did not welcome him. Yet some people accepted him and put their faith in him. So he gave them the right to be the children of God. They were not God's children by nature or because of any human desires. God himself was the one who made them his children" (John 1:11-13 CEV).

Why did Jesus go through so much trouble, suffer such enormous pain, and pay so great a price? Because of His love for humanity. He loves us and became our servant in order to save us from our sins. As the world gets meaner and uglier, Christ is creating a people who are meek and humble. God is building a new family on earth, designed to be a part of His heritage, and springing from His seed. Within it, He has ordained offspring who will honor Him as Father. In the Lord Jesus Christ, there are no broken relationships. His children are brothers and sisters. If there is a visual illustration of what makes this portrait of His creation so glorious, it is the different colors and shades of people being merged into a grand mosaic of tribes, tongues, and nations. All are the object of His love and a reflection of His face. The beauty of God's family is like sun rays filtering through a dense forest, splashing down their warm, bejeweled beams upon the rainwater resting on the leaves of a flower before finding oneness in the stream below. The care He has for this new family of His on earth mystifies the angels and magnifies His universal glory.

The Family Name

The one thing that can dull the glow of God's radiance is for His children to act like strangers. When the brothers and sisters of the Lord's family turn away or reject one another, they give His family a bad name. Imagine what it must look like to the world to stand on the outside, looking in on God's family each Sunday morning, and to observe them bickering and fighting with or segregated from one another. Like undisciplined children running around in public places, it must lead them to wonder, "Whose children did you say these were?"

As God's family, we are called to protect the family name. We are to honor Him, live for Him, and exhibit His qualities. The Lord even promised the disciples that the rest of the world would see God in their behavior if they would love each other. Imagine that—your neighborhood recognizes the Lord in you when they observe you loving your brothers and sisters in Christ. On the other hand, when they see us rejecting each other and fighting among ourselves, they must assume God is not present in our midst.

"Father, make them one," Jesus prays in John 17, "so that the world may believe that You sent Me." *He would be pleased if we put aside our prejudices and predispositions and got to know each other for the sake of His name.* He wants us to make the commitment to treat each other as brothers— not merely as friends and neighbors. He desires us to be committed to one another as family. That means the old arguments about the church being made up of "homogeneous units"—people from the same income bracket, the same neighborhood, or the same ethnic background—is not what God had in mind. In His omniscience and wisdom, He made us different, and He expects us to be brothers in spite of our differences.

I remember my mama saying to me, "Boy, if you get out there and start acting a fool, don't tell 'em I'm your mama!" In other words, she expected me to protect her good reputation in the community. In a similar way, the apostles of Jesus were very careful to protect the name of their Father. We are to do likewise.

Most children fail to realize that everything they do affects their entire family, whether they want it to or not.

We are a part of the family of God. Every member ought to have a vested interest in each other. Failure to have a genuine concern is a cause for alarm. It would be like your own body showing disregard for another part of itself. A child who is rejected by his brothers lives in a dysfunctional family, and *God doesn't expect His family to be dysfunctional!*

Supernatural Life

Some people will probably argue with me that I'm taking the notion of God's family too far. To them, the only true family relationships are natural—that is, you were born into them. Such was the case of Cain and Abel. But if you are a Christian, you have been born again, born into a new family. I firmly believe the Lord created the natural family to be the divine pattern upon which a healthy society exists. At the same time, I believe He intends for this divine pattern of relationships to be the model of community that all believers are to pursue. God is not going to alter His plan due to the inability of man to see the genius of His scheme and come together. A naturally special bond should exist between members of God's family. Therefore, as His children, we are to "continue to love each other with true brotherly love," according to Hebrews 13:1 (TLB).

The natural family may be your first experience, but it is not the only family you have, it is merely an introduction. As a believer, you belong to a spiritual family whose boundaries of love and forgiveness transcend those of a natural family because the heart of God is alive in your bosom. If you truly want to live as a healthy member of His family, it will require a commitment to the same behaviors it takes to have a healthy physical family: selflessness, dependability, and a genuine concern for one another. Are you really interested in living the supernatural life? Then learn to put others first. Jesus said, "If anyone would come after me, he must deny himself" (Matthew 16:24 NIV). In order to draw upon the life of God to enable you to live as Christ did, self-denial is a prerequisite. You must practice putting others first, esteeming them as higher than yourself. That's what happens in a loving family, and it's what should characterize our lives as Christians.

Loving a brother is a natural by-product of loving God. The supernatural life grows as the natural life fades. Before the supernatural can increase in a man's life, the natural must decrease. So make a commitment to your brothers to see them as family. Make an effort to offer your help when needed. Demonstrate your concern, don't just talk about it. The family of God would be very different if each of us were to take to heart Paul's prescription to try and outdo each other in love.

It's never easy to develop a loving family. There are prejudices and problems to overcome. There will be brothers and sisters you don't like, and some who will reject your attempts at help. Worse, there will be a few who will use you, accepting your assistance but never offering a word of thanks. It's hard to face those situations when they arise, but it's important that we remember the principle which overcomes the problem: *We are a family.* Just because someone acts poorly toward us doesn't make them any less family. As it is in your natural family, so it is with the family of God. In due time, our Father will respond to their foolishness, if necessary.

A few years ago I was astonished upon reading in the *Los Angeles Times* the story of a woman found homeless and living on the streets of Orange County. She had no possessions, only the clothes on her back, and she was hungry. Like thousands of others across the country, she was a woman without hope. That in itself is not necessarily the stuff of which headlines are made. But there is more to her story. She was an heiress to a vast fortune. She was related to members of the royal family in Britain. She had plenty of connections who could easily have helped her. But she was living as a pauper on the streets of Los Angeles because she was sick and displaced.

Brother, scattered about us are heirs to the kingdom of God. More than royal inhabitants of a nation, they are citizens of heaven, lost and living on the streets of spiritual poverty. But they are our brothers and sisters in Christ. It is our natural responsibility to recognize them as family. Will you do your part? Will you reach out to them and welcome them into our Father's house?

18

Learning to Be Family

When the average man asks "How are you?" he is usually not searching for information. He is making polite conversation. Therefore he doesn't expect an in-depth, or even a particularly honest response. That is just the way of the world. Does he really care? Perhaps, but suppose you were to respond, "Things are mighty rough right now." Do you think he would hear you? Don't be surprised or upset if he comes back with, "That's good." Your response never registered with him in the first place. He wasn't interested in anything but an answer like, "I'm fine!"

In today's society, "How are you?" is just another way of saying "Hello" or "What's up?" It is a common expression of simple courtesy, nothing more. Maybe during some period in the past it meant more, but today it usually means, "If you have a problem, please don't tell me." Most people do not have the time nor the inclination to listen. Loving someone takes time and energy.

According to the Bible, we are created to love God, but the evidence that we do is demonstrated by how we love others. As you grow in your relationships with your brothers in Christ, you mature spiritually. But if you can't develop those relationships, it is probably because growing up you didn't learn the meaning of family. The natural family is the laboratory in which we first began to practice love. It's no wonder the family of God—the church—is so messed up. The laboratory is a wreck!

"Familyhood"

The common expressions depicting a family in the world today include "family feud," "family violence," and "family squabble" (i.e., the Hatfields and the McCoys). Our culture is racked with more domestic violence than domestic bliss, more sibling rivalry than brotherly love. Psychologists say such behavior is "natural." That is what our children tried to convince us of as they were growing up feuding.

"Well, Dad," they would begin, "it seems like everybody but you and Mom know it's natural for siblings to fuss and fight." My wife and I refused to buy into that lie, and we insisted on fostering family unity. While most people talk about their "neighborhood," we started talking about our "familyhood." Today in our house, holidays, birthdays, and special events are increasingly becoming just another excuse for the family to get together and have fun. It's not perfect, but it is wonderful.

How do you go from feuding to fun?

Bunny and I had to seek a loftier place upon which to build our family than simply relying on our surname. The fact that they were born into the same household didn't seem to overcome the children's learned tendencies to bicker with one another and insist upon their own way. So we tried to develop a sense of interdependence with one another, seeking the best for a brother or sister. We turned to the principles of family buried in the fertile soil of the Word of God. We found His wisdom lodged deep within the kernels of His eternal truth.

"Can't we all just get along?" wasn't working in our family, so we started to apply constant reminders of what we mean to each other and who we are in the kingdom as His representatives on earth. My children are not just brothers and sisters in the Wilson family...they are ambassadors for the family of God. Several years have passed, and I can see clearly now the power of His Word and the reason why God is building a new family. It benefits everyone. The world sees His grace and love in the actions of one brother to another. They observe His faithfulness and mercy in the helping hand one sister offers another.

In one grand, sweeping statement regarding man's relationship to man, Abraham summarized the heart of the matter: "Let's not have any quarreling between you and me," he said to his nephew Lot in Genesis 13:8 (NIV), "or between your herdsmen and mine, for we are brothers."

When I read those words, it was as though Abraham were standing at the very edge of human reasoning, looking across the boundaries of the temporary and seeing the eternal. He was able to get beyond himself, past the apex of his own painstakingly gained plateaus, and catch a small glimpse of the boundlessness of the kingdom of God. With a world ripe for the taking, Abraham graciously let his brother choose first.

A Family Tie

Jesus told His followers the greatest commandment was that a man ought to love the Lord with all his heart, soul, mind, and strength. He went on to note that the second commandment is like the first: A man should love his neighbor as himself. In those two simple commands, Christ summed up the basics of the Christian life. When a man loves God and loves his neighbor, he is living out the faith. He is fulfilling the law of Christ.

Abraham, the father of Israel, put into practice that greatest commandment, loving God by loving his brother. Lot had traveled with his uncle from Haran, the land of their dwelling, to Canaan, the land of their destiny. Though Lot chose to accompany Abraham and Sarah on this mysterious journey, at the very least he must have had a million and one questions tugging at the fringes of his mind. "Where will we go? When will we arrive? What will it be like?"

After leaving Haran and traveling for years, Abraham became very rich in livestock, silver, and gold. Yet he never forgot to worship God. From time to time he would return to the place called Bethel, where he had left a heap of stones he had erected as an altar of prayer, and give thanks. Wealth and success were his, but Abraham remembered that it had only come because of God's grace, not through his own ability. We ought to be anxious to worship God when we remember His greatness and His goodness to us. And it should fan within us a fire of faith and an ear eager to hear and obey His voice.

But Abraham was not the only one gaining wealth, for Lot also had acquired "flocks and herds and tents," according to Genesis 13:5. Coincidence? Not at all. As Proverbs 13:20 (NIV) says, "He who walks with the wise grows wise, but a companion of fools suffers harm." Lot learned from watching his uncle, and grew wealthy by following the godly pattern of Abraham. Both men had amassed huge herds of livestock, and their herdsmen were beginning to squabble among themselves. Abraham sought to resolve the matter quickly before it could get out of hand. They had moved into an area that was sur-rounded by the Canaanites and the Perizzites—two different groups of people who worshiped false deities—and

Abraham seized upon the opportunity to let his light shine in the midst of the darkness. He said to his nephew, "We are brothers. Let's not fight, but figure out a plan that will be beneficial for both of us."

His entire manner was selfless. He thought of Lot's success, and he desired to help his nephew as much as possible, so Abraham stood on a hill with the younger man and said, "Take a look. You go whichever way you want, and I'll go the other. That way we won't have our people fighting. We'll always be brothers, and I want what's best for you, so choose what you think is best." In saying those words, Abraham sacrificed what rightfully belonged to him. He thought it important to not diminish the sanctity of the God they represented. Abraham gave Lot first choice in selecting the land he desired, and told his brother he would settle for what remained.

I used to be bothered by this arrangement, because the promise from God was made to Abraham, not Lot. Then I realized God had given the land to Abraham already, so he was free to give it away if he so chose. Abraham was confident in the fact that He who promised it was also the same One who would provide it.

Oswald Chambers, in his widely read devotional *My Utmost for His Highest*, states that Abraham waived his rights and left the choice to God. In return, God blessed Abraham with an even greater abundance.

Character Reveals Itself

One thing I've learned about business associates is that, sooner or later, a man's character reveals itself. If he is greedy, his greed will soon evidence itself. If he is honest, it will become clear that he always tells the truth. I believe that Abraham's character was evident in the offer he made to his brother. He was selfless, mature, and concerned about the needs of the younger man. In offering him the choice, Abraham was willing to consider the welfare of another.

I think we often have the opportunity and the resources to help a brother in need, then choose to fall back on a street mentality that says, "He needs to get his the way I got mine." That guy could have the same success I've had if he worked as hard as I've worked." Unfortunately, that attitude doesn't convey the love and caring of Christ. Loving a brother as a family member means helping him when you have the opportunity to do so. Abraham had that attitude.

Unfortunately, we also begin to get a glimpse into the character of Lot. Here is a young man who should be thanking the Lord for his godly uncle. If he had a proper sense of respect, he would have bowed down in humility before Abraham and insisted his elder select first. Instead, he selfishly chose the best land for himself. In spite of the fact that he was Abraham's guest, Lot chose to think of his own needs rather than the needs of his uncle. In doing so, Lot revealed his character. He thought of himself first. Perhaps it's not surprising that Lot would later offer his daughters to sexually immoral men, fail to influence his sons- in-law for the Lord, and end up sleeping with his own daughters in a drunken stupor.

I can see Abraham not only shining a light for his neighbors to see God's family in operation, but teaching his relatives the proper platform for their divine heritage. Lot needed to know how to represent the Father by faith in the face of contrary facts. In Abraham, he had a brother with whom he could spend time and from whom he could learn.

Sometimes we are prone to walk away from those we are closest to, due to our disappointments in them. But we must not abandon them, for God would not abandon us. Abraham probably sensed Lot was making a mistake, but they remained brothers. There is a lesson for us in that. *We must seize every opportunity to demonstrate our Father's character to our culture.*

In the city where Lot and his family had moved, an armed rebellion broke out. Lot and his family were among the host of prisoners taken captive. Immediately upon hearing of it, Abraham commanded his 300 servants to go with him on a rescue mission. It is likely that at least one of them thought, "I can't believe we're risking our lives to go rescue that greedy Lot and his family!" But Abraham did exactly that, triumphing in battle and gaining the release of his nephew and all the confiscated goods.

Lot should have wanted to know at least one thing from Abraham, especially after he had chosen the most fertile and well-watered land along the Jordan plains, after he had shown an attraction to worldly living, and been silent in witnessing his faith to his neighbors. Lot should have looked at his uncle and asked, "Why did you risk everything to come and rescue me?"

Abraham's answer no doubt would have been, "I thought you already knew. It is because we are brothers."

Loving God and Others

Life has many ways of kidnapping a person, and it helps to have a brother willing to lead some friends on a rescue mission. My friend Dayne owned a very successful telephone installation company, yet after a new marriage, a change of careers, and some terrible choices, he needed the fellowship of brothers more than ever. He says now, "I was a mess—drinking, doing drugs, abusing my family. I'll never forget coming home high one night, only to find Frank and some other brothers in my living room. They told my family to leave the room and not re-enter, then these guys got in my face.

"I wanted to leave, but these men wouldn't let me run away. They stayed with me through the night, until I came to myself and repented. By getting in my face they challenged me to deal with the fear I had of failing, the confusion of changes required in relationships, and elevating the cares of my mate above my own selfish needs. In taking the action these men took, they showed me they weren't just saying the words 'I love you,' they were demonstrating it.

"My brothers showed me to what lengths they were willing to go to love me. Having godly men in my life, holding me accountable for my Christian walk, keeps me in check. My reverent fear of God, my love and respect for my wife, and an awakening to how I can impact my community all blossomed because my brothers were willing to challenge my personal choices.

"On earth we demonstrate our relationship to God by how we treat each other. That is the sign which identifies us as His family. My brothers demonstrated Jesus Christ to me that night."

Where can a man learn to love God in that manner? In a selfish, sin-soaked world, how does a man learn to put others first? What does he do in order to begin caring for others? If you ponder those questions for a moment, you'll soon realize that Christ has given us a tough task. It isn't *natural* to think about the needs of someone else. The *natural* thing to do is to consider your own needs first. But in Jesus Christ, we are given *supernatural* power to love others. Simply stated, when we recognize how much God loves us and how much He has done on our behalf, we recognize that we owe it to Him to obey. Simply stated, when we see Christ's example, we begin to follow it and "love our neighbors as ourselves."

Your neighbor is the one in need nearest you. It could be a family member, a friend, or a perfect stranger, as was the case in the story of the good Samaritan (Luke 10:30-37). Try putting yourself in your neighbor's predicament for a moment and respond to him or her the way you would want someone to respond if you were the one in need. Trust me, this requires practice. Begin with someone you already know and love, with the brother to whom you have entrusted your friendship. And remember the words of King Solomon: "There is a friend who sticks closer than a brother" (Proverbs 18:24). Start there and see what the Lord would have you do. If a man would have friends, he must show himself friendly.

19
We Need
Each Other

Leonard and I used to work together in the record business as co-writers and producers on some of Motown's key artists, up until the day I left the industry. Leonard had committed his life to Christ, and a few years later had started coming to our men's gathering at the restaurant each Thursday morning.

One thing I knew about Leonard was that he had never realized true satisfaction in his career. Regardless of the number of hit records he had earned, he felt they had always been "shared" with another, so he did not have the "success" he felt he deserved. I cannot say for certain why Leonard felt like that—he was a musical genius— perhaps it had something to do with his family background, his lack of a stationary father figure, and the years he spent growing up on welfare in the tenement slums of Chicago's south side.

His journey carried him through four generations of family members being trapped in the vicious, life-draining cycle of welfare. Leonard made it out, but no one ever gave him credit for doing so. He spent the next several years paying for his success, trying to buy the respect of those who seemed to least appreciate it—particularly those closest to him. Because of this, he was never quite able to enjoy the sweet taste of his own accomplishments. Eventually, he set out on a deadly course of self-destruction. At the Thursday morning fellowships, he always knew the right thing to say, quoted the right Scriptures, and offered some nice-sounding prayers. But they were all a part of an elaborate masquerade. Leonard's mask was so skillfully set into place that at times his own wife could not tell the difference between his real face and a false front.

Committed to Honesty

You see, walking together in a committed relationship requires honesty. That is not to say Leonard was being purposefully dishonest, because all of us were there for the same reason—to learn how to love one another. But I believe he was hiding from himself. He still felt like a failure and wouldn't let on. He was extremely knowledgeable about many subjects, but often when he saw himself trapped by a question for which he had no answer, it appeared that he would simply play word games and create confusion so as not to seem intellectually or spiritually inferior. Eventually his work opportunities ground to a halt, leaving little escape from his numbing fear of failure.

Still he maintained a vigilant gaze onto that next level of achievement—the one with his name alone perched upon its lofty ledge. But it was to no avail. It was as though the door of opportunity was bolted shut and no one had left a key for him. Gradually, Leonard discontinued attending the morning men's fellowship. We began to call him, but rarely got a response. One day I ran into his wife, who admitted to me, "Leonard is doing drugs, Frank. Most of the time he either stays out all night or comes home during the early hours of the morning after I have left for work." Here was a brother in need. I asked her to give me a call the next time she knew he was home.

About two weeks later, as she was on her way out the door for work, she called and whispered, "He's home now." Not knowing what to expect, I armed myself with God's Word. What I encountered was not totally unfamiliar—I had seen drug problems many times in the world with some of my associates and their friends in the entertainment industry. What I did not expect to find was a man stripped of his dignity and completely devoid of pride, sitting at his kitchen table, nodding back and forth in a drug-induced stupor. I didn't know what to say. Maybe just my being there said it all: "I'm with you rain or shine."

Leonard survived. We got him the help he needed, he turned his life around, and today he and his family are stronger than ever. He is now a leader within the ministry of a fast-growing northeastern congregation, and he is helping others overcome feelings of rejection and get a new start in life. The fact that he had brothers and a wife who never gave up on him was one of the key factors in Leonard's life changing.

The Price of Ambition

Demone was a fast-talking young Puerto Rican kid from the Bronx who came to my attention at a Christian Entertainer's Fellowship luncheon. The first thing he did after introducing himself was to demonstrate his mastery of hip-hop and rap—without wondering if anyone would be listening. He had arrived in Hollywood intent upon taking the entertainment industry by storm as a rapper and producer of hip-hop music. Due to his skills as a communicator, Demone immediately talked himself into a front-office position at a rising hip-hop club in the city.

He started out well, but due to a downturn in the fortunes of the club, he soon fell upon hard times.

He was smart, but did far more talking than he did walking. His gift of gab enabled him to talk himself into many deals, but he had a difficult time delivering the goods. It was always one project after another, one momentous event after another, until you just did not want to hear about any more of his brainstorms. During the process of rebounding, Demone met someone who told him about knowing the Lord. Realizing this was what he needed most in his life, Demone committed his life to Christ and set sail toward an assault on the world of Christian music. In his mind, a brash young Puerto Rican lad would be performing gospel hip-hop and taking it to the streets.

One day Demone called, saying that God had told him to purchase a bus and embark upon a national tour to the street kids across America. He had a couple of CDs out and was excited as he made plans for the trip. I talked with him briefly and encouraged him to pray over his decision, but Demone was set in his thinking: He was going to be a star for Jesus.

Six months later, I got a call. Demone was in jail, trying to raise bail money. He hadn't been able to handle the stress of all the concerns over lodging, food, automotive repairs, bookings, and the million details it takes for a tour. Eventually he got caught up with the wrong element and began to smoke crack. It wasn't the first time he had been in trouble, and we were afraid the judge would come down hard on Demone.

Together with his pastor, we reached out to his court-appointed public defender. With a bit of help, he was given a light sentence of one year, mandatory drug treatment, and a stern warning from the judge. With good behavior and time already served, Demone could be back on the streets in six months.

A Restless Night

Late one night, as I was lying in bed about six months later, I was stirred in my spirit to get up, get dressed, and drive down Fair Oaks Avenue. I didn't know what it was, but I got up and drove up and down that street for an hour. That's when I saw him, standing on the corner, waiting for something.

"Demone!" I called out. Recognizing who I was, he quickly rushed over to the passenger side of my car and said, "Boy, am I glad to see you. What are you doing out this time of the night?"

"Looking for you, I guess," I told him. I didn't know what to do next, until it dawned on me that I ought to introduce Demone to Leonard. It was one o'clock in the morning, but I grabbed my cell phone and called my friend. His wife, Carolyn, answered the phone and I nervously inquired, "Is Leonard asleep?"

"No," she explained, "he's out in his studio." Shortly after, he was on the phone and inviting us over for a visit.

As soon as we sat down in Leonard's studio, Demone began telling us both about his latest idea, which he came up with while sitting in the slammer. I prevailed upon him to shut up and listen for a minute. "Leonard, I just picked this brother up at a street corner, where he was released after doing six months for possession of drugs and a parole violation. I felt he shouldn't spend one more night on earth without hearing from you."

With those words, Leonard heaved a sigh and began to tell his story. "I was in bondage, son. I had left my family and moved into a house with Crips who were dealing drugs, just so I could sell it and make a little extra money to afford my own habit. One day, as I was stretched out on the floor, I could hear my little boy calling my name. You see, every evening on the way home from work, my wife picked him up from school and they would have to drive right past that house on their way home. On this particular day, they spotted my car in front of a group of duplexes. Not knowing exactly where I was, he frantically pulled on her coat sleeve and begged, 'Stop the car, Mom!' She did, and my little boy jumped out and began to run between the different houses, calling out at the top of his lungs, 'Daddy, Daddy, Daddy!' He was just nine years old.

"It was the lowest point in my life. The echo from the sound of my son's voice kept knifing deeper and deeper into my soul. God used it to pull me to freedom. I had to look at my life and ask, 'What am I doing here? What am I doing to my children?'

"When I reached for help, it was my brothers God used. They were there; they cared for me and helped me change my life." Then, as I sat praying quietly for Demone, Leonard looked at him and asked, "What are you doing here, Demone? Where might your life be headed?"

That night changed Demone's path. He sat quietly and listened, and for the first time since I had met him, he didn't say one word. Today Demone is on full-time staff at his local church, working in the media department and with the youth in his community. The Bible says, "Two are better than one, because they have a good reward for their labor. For if they fall, one will lift up his companion. But woe to him who is alone when he falls for he has no one to help him up" (Ecclesiastes 4:9,10). I'm glad on that night I had a brother I was walking with who could explain the woes of falling down. I don't think I could have helped Demone by myself, but with my brother Leonard being used by the Lord, we were able to reach him.

Everyone Needs Someone

The important thing to remember is this: We each need someone. Every Christian, male and female, needs someone who has a license to challenge our commitment. Each of us needs someone brave enough to get in our face and say, "That's not right." We all want to have someone close enough to bounce ideas off, or to ask an honest opinion of, or to share a wild dream with. A relationship with a friend with whom we are not in competition on any level. In other words, a brother.

Your brother knows that when you win, he wins. He's not jealous. You're on the same team, and God is your Captain. Oh, for the privilege of walking with a brother who is committed to God, and who is committed to you! What rare good fortune! Is there a brother who can speak a word that challenges you concerning anything he has observed in your life, without offending you? The visible sign of redemption is demonstrated by the wholeness in your relationship with God, and by your unconditional commitment to another person.

King David's natural brother rejected him because of his jealousy and private fear. Perhaps he should have been open enough to walk with his brother and learn from David the secret of courage and the power of praise. Instead, he was content to be an envious, spiritually lukewarm sibling, slowly slipping into obscurity.

Jonathan, on the other hand, recognized in David a kindred spirit, and made with him a covenant of friendship and brotherhood. Jonathan admired and trusted David. He could see in their relationship a greater potential for his own growth. Certainly you can look back on your own life and recognize kindred spirits—those with whom you share a love for the Lord, a commitment to His kingdom, and a desire for a closer walk. Although you might not be able to put your finger on it, you know there is a divine connection between the two of you, and it was initiated in heaven.

God has sent someone to join you on your spiritual sojourn. They will wrestle with you, help you to break away from the tendencies of the past, and assist you when you fall. Why remain content to live an ordinary existence of self-absorption and stunted spiritual growth when you can have a deeper, richer relationship in Jesus Christ? The truth of the matter is this: *We need each other.* In order to become what God wants us to be, we need our brothers. And the Lord has sent us on a mission to drive that point home.

20
A Sight for Sore Eyes

There was a time when if a man gave you his word, you could take it to the bank. Now it is more likely you will have to take him to court. What changed?

Well, if you ask the average man if he keeps his promises, he will no doubt answer in the affirmative. Yet, it is said by many that man's moral compass today is no longer an accurate indicator of reality.

"Gradually," they say, "he seems to have drifted away from a standard that is grounded in the Word of God, to a wishy-washiness of suppositions." If that is true, and I believe in some instances it is, we have to set the record straight!

Brothers, we need one another to help us become what God says we already are: "...a new creation" in Christ. Together, let us call men back to that place where our word is our bond, our effort is our best, and where we help keep each other strong. Dare men attempt to keep their walk straight, their eyes on heaven, and their women on a pedestal? That would be a sight for sore eyes.

Most of all, we will stand with one another through adversity, for that is what we were born to do.

Living In Adversity

It was approximately 6:45 in the morning when Rich, walking at a brisk pace, pushed open the heavy glass doors like a man on a mission. We had not seen him at the fellowship for at least nine months. Rich was a very busy man, heading one of the largest music publishing companies in America. He was right at home hobnobbing with the millionaire jet-setters of the world. But he had slowly drifted away from our group. His attendance became erratic, and eventually he dropped out completely.

I knew our fellowship group had had a big impact on Rich's life, but for some reason he had chosen to slide away from us. It was quite a surprise to see him ambling toward the restaurant where we met each week.

Not knowing we had relocated to another section of the restaurant, Rich came through the doors and quickly turned right, heading into the area where we normally sat. There was no one there—unknown to him, the restaurant had decided to move us to another part of the building in order to accommodate our growing numbers. I was situated in such a way that I could see Rich as he came through the doors, but he couldn't see me. As he walked in and surveyed the empty room, his entire body language reflected disappointment and pain. Tears began to cloud his eyes as he whirled around to leave. Since there were other people enjoying their early-morning breakfasts at the restaurant, we didn't feel we could holler out to Rich. So we waited until we could get his attention.

Just as he turned to exit the building, he caught a glimpse of 50 hands waving at him, revealing our new location. With a smile, Rich hurried to the set of tables where our group was seated and exhaled a huge sigh of relief. "You brothers are a sight for sore eyes," he told us. "I thought you had stopped getting together."

Taking his seat slowly, Rich proceeded to share how his life was falling apart, his marriage was on the verge of collapse, his spiritual life was in tatters, and his job—not willing to be outdone by the other troubles—was becoming more than he could manage. Rich had been married more than 15 years and was blessed with three beautiful children. The routine of making new publishing deals, interviewing and signing new talents, all the while playing nursemaid to disgruntled writers and staffers, had gutted the insides of the man. He felt obligated to produce more and more bottom-line profits. The responsibility was taking him away from his family too much and adversely affecting his health.

On top of that, the temptation of seeing a consistent parade of beautiful women at business and social functions was not lessening the pressure he was feeling. Rich had decided that being the head of a large company mandated his presence at nearly every event related to his business. It is easy to get caught up in the rat race and not be conscious of the fact that somebody else is setting out cheese to trap you. All that we call blessings in life do not necessarily come from God—sometimes they can be the predator's bait, placed just beyond our grasp and connected to his trap, waiting for us to bite. Once you're in the enemy's clutches, he laughs and considers you defeated.

Trouble—The Identifier of Friends

The best thing that can happen in a situation like that is for a brother to walk close with you. He can come alongside and help you out, even if it places him at risk. "A friend loves at all times, and a brother is born for adversity," the Bible tells us. If that Scripture looks strange to you, perhaps it is because you have had no real brothers in your life, just distant relatives. Remember, we are strangers when we are born. We *learn* to be brothers.

In the case of Rich, we had enjoyed great fellowship in the past and were spiritually connected. That morning we had spent consoling Clovis, another brother who was experiencing a difficult situation. His only son had come home and reported that his teacher, a popular male instructor at his school, had sexually molested him. The employee had since been suspended and arrested, but was currently out on bail. Clovis was angry, frustrated, and in need of some brotherly concern and advice.

Some of the brothers coming to the morning fellowship were new converts, still rough around the edges, and they were so incensed over Clovis's situation that they were instantly ready to attack the perpetrator—even if it meant going to jail themselves. But we calmed everybody down and got into a great discussion of forgiveness and accountability. To be sure, we all felt Clovis's pain, his anger, and his own sense of guilt for not being there to protect his son. A few of the brothers committed themselves to devoting extra time in standing with Clovis, making certain he did nothing that would make matters worse. We helped him get through the hardest parts of the ordeal.

Rich was deeply touched by our discussion. He found himself agreeing with our position, and settled down to listen quietly as supernatural wisdom flowed from the mouths of spiritually mature, biblically grounded brothers. His own problems subsided significantly as he contrasted his own situation with that of Clovis. As the conversation turned toward his own problems, he realized that trouble is a common criminal. The brothers began sharing their personal disappointments, failures, and triumphs. Then they prayed for him and watched the weight of his anxieties lift, and a fresh anointing of his own faith released within him. Rich walked out of that meeting a new man and was reminded of the strength that comes from walking closely with a group of other men.

A Wise Man

The Lord expects us to read His Word and obey it. He also expects us to listen to the wise men He has placed around us, in order to gain a new perspective on our problems. Once, when talking with my friends in Washington, DC, we were joined by a man who was fighting for his political life. He was running for statewide office in South Carolina, and his political enemies were laying vicious traps for him left and right. His name was being scandalized, attempts were made to set him up with disreputable women, and his office's campaign fund-raising efforts were being stymied. Money was drying up quickly, and in politics these days, money drives a campaign.

As we listened to this brother lament his trials, he suddenly looked up and asked, "What do you men think I should I do?" My friend Gene Browning amazed me with his fast reply: "Brother, a prudent man sees danger coming and hides himself. But the fool walks right into it and is punished."

It turns out the man had been given some opportunities to attack back. He felt it was a dangerous approach, but his natural inclination was to do just that. As we began discussing the biblical prescriptions for him, however, it became clear the Lord wouldn't want one of His children attacking someone. This man had never thought of his situation in quite that light before. Rather than going on the attack, he chose to be like Jesus and simply respond in humility and grace. Win or lose, he was going to reflect the love of God in his campaign.

Knowing wise men allows you to be able to find wisdom when you need it. Knowing God's Word allows you to be able to share wisdom when someone else needs it. The Lord Jesus, when facing the devil's temptations, relied on Scripture to protect Himself. We ought to do the same. I decided right then and there to fill my mind with

Bible verses, so that when brothers came to me for advice, I could rely on the very thoughts of God. I want to share the Lord's wisdom with a brother in trouble, not just my own. Although my friend lost the election, he was immediately invited to sit on one of the most powerful boards in America.

Walking Together

Cleveland had one of the hottest shows on television for quite some time, but for reasons unknown he never saw himself as a success. For months he had been a regular part of the Thursday morning men's group, then one day we noticed he had not been attending for a while. When we called, his brother told us that Cleve had gotten back into his old cocaine habit. We decided to take action that very day, and a few of us paid him a brotherly visit.

When we arrived at his home, Cleve looked like he had been through a storm. He was unshaven, uncombed, in need of a bath, and unable to walk straight without holding onto something. He had always been a very sharp dresser, and to see him this way told us that Cleveland was slipping into the abyss. Facing him, we began praying for Cleve, who sobbed heavily. He thanked us for caring enough to come and minister to him. Our presence demonstrated our love for him. *In walking together, especially with a brother in crisis, we deliberately identify ourselves with God's interest in others.*

A Lone Ranger is an easy prey for a pack of wolves. If one doesn't get you, another one usually will. And what else are shame, fear, guilt, and feelings of insignificance and inadequacy? They are nothing other than a pack of wild animals. And pride itself is nothing but a wolf in sheep's clothing. And all of them are dangerous.

When I look back over the reasons why our Thursday men's fellowship grew so fast, I think it's because we all saw lives changing. Even though it met at 6:00 A.M., men were rushing to get there, and to get there on time. Women were pushing their husbands out of bed because they did not want their spouses to miss it, not even for one morning. Marriages were changing, families were being healed and made healthier. Single guys were listening to the voices of experience. Two young men, Mario and Paul, sat there every Thursday morning for more than two years without saying a word, paying attention to the mature men in the group.

Our section in the restaurant began drawing some of the other patrons from within the restaurant who wanted to find out what we were doing. They would see our Bibles open on the tables and want to listen in on our discussions. Were the men attending because of the discussions? No. Did they come to pray? No, though we often did that when men needed prayer. Were they showing up because we were studying the Bible? No. Bible studies were everywhere, and they could certainly find a nicer location and a more convenient time. So what was the attraction?

We were there, encouraging each other and spurring one another on to love and good works. We were complimenting rather than competing against one another. We care for our brothers. We were trying to outdo one another, but in love. It was just men together, and for many men that is a sight for sore eyes.

21
A Time to Love

Two Greeks journeyed to Jerusalem for the annual celebration of the Passover. All of the talk in the city was about the miraculous ministry of Jesus, about His compassion and capabilities. Philip and Andrew told the Master about the strangers' request to see Him. I found His response to be most puzzling.

Jesus said, "The hour has come for the Son of Man to be glorified." After having reviewed this passage for a while, I now see that an addendum to His specific message is possible without doing harm to its meaning. His glorification would lead to His multiplication. It is reminiscent of what happened when He took two fish and five barley loaves of bread, broke them, and fed 5000 men as well as all of the women and the children. His broken body was to be multiplied in like manner. "Most assuredly I say to you, unless a grain of wheat falls into the ground and dies, it remains alone; but if it dies, it produces much grain" (John 12:23,24).

Jesus is saying to us that through His death and resurrection, He is going to harvest Himself in the souls of so many people that those who hunger to see Him, experience His loving touch, and hear His comforting words of salvation and safety will only need to encounter the Christ who indwells the Christian. His love will be evident in their actions. A relative principle is lifted from the laws of the old covenant: The poor were to be great beneficiaries of the people of God.

God instructed Moses to tell Israel, "When you reap the harvest of your land, you shall not wholly reap the corners of your field, nor shall you gather the gleanings of your harvest. And you shall not glean your vineyard; you shall leave them for the poor and the stranger: I am the LORD your God" (Leviticus 19:9,10).

The Lord went on to instruct His people: "It shall be for the stranger, the fatherless, and the widow, that the LORD your God may bless you in all the work of your hands" (Deuteronomy 24:19). In other words, God's people were to care for others. Now those of us who are of the new covenant bear the same privilege because God's laws are written upon the tablets of our hearts through His Holy Spirit. His agenda is foremost on our minds.

Born to Be a Lover

So it was with some interest that I recently read an article that quoted former United Nations ambassador Andrew Young saying, "In a society based on free enterprise, poverty is too expensive to tolerate."

My reaction was, "Poverty, you say?" To see the poor in America, we have to go where they live, and most of us aren't interested. Besides, the real poverty in this country is not monetary poverty, but spiritual poverty. The condition comes from a lack of concern for people. What we are experiencing is a poverty of love. There simply is not enough love to go around, it would seem. To continue being advised of the suffering of those who are forced to live without the things most of us take for granted, and then to go on as if nothing were wrong, would suggest to me that I may be dead and not know it. If I want to really show people God, I'll reflect His love.

My Father God is love. His children are born to be lovers. Whether Mother Teresa was a saint or not is debatable, but that she was the embodiment of the love of God is indisputable. It is precisely what God accomplished through Jesus, giving birth to children who are fleshing out His character in their daily lives.

You were born to be a lover. Who are you loving? Who is loving you?

Starting Over

Here is how we can recognize the difference between God's offspring and Satan's. John says, "In this the children of God and the children of the devil are manifest: Whoever does not practice righteousness is not of God, nor is he who does not love his brother" (1 John 3:10). *How can I learn to love another brother as God says to love him? By changing how I see him.* Instead of seeing another man as my competitor for a dwindling resource or a potential threat to my personal well-being, I should see him as another child the Father loves, just as He loves me.

When I was growing up in a big family in Houston, everybody went to the dinner table with an agenda. Most of us competed for the chicken breast or the drumsticks and thighs. The wings went next. Whoever was late for the meal was the loser, because he was left with nothing but the gristly chicken feet and bony neck (by then even the back would have been claimed!). There may have been lots of laughter in our house on some occasions, but those days when everyone showed up on time for dinner were not funny. It was competition—he with the fastest hands wins.

As we matured, we learned to take turns sharing the most desirable parts. We appreciated my mother's culinary skills at making the less-prominent portions just as delicious, and believed that one day we would have enough of everything for everyone to enjoy. That is a lesson we strive to teach our children today.

Learning to give up something for another person is part of the maturing process. While we were still living at home with our parents, we never grew to the point where we could subordinate our desires consistently and allow each other to have the best part without a discussion, but every once in a while, we did. Because after all, we were family.

Likewise, as we graciously give away to others a portion of what we desire to keep for ourselves, we are sharing with them the best part of us: God's love. When we appreciate another person as one of the Father's children, it prompts us to pray more earnestly for His wisdom in seeking to raise the quality of life for all of those in His family, not just the ones we call brothers. It cultivates within us the attitude that in God's economy we are all winners.

The apostle Paul said, "I have learned to be satisfied with what I have. I know what it is to be in need, and what it is to have more than enough. I have learned this secret, so that anywhere, at any time, I am content. . . . I have the strength to face all conditions by the power that Christ gives me" (Philippians 4:11-13 TEV). Paul understood that sometimes the best thing is to let someone else win. When was the last time you took that approach?

The Challenge

Loving your brothers and sisters in Christ is crucial if we are going to change the world. Why do I place so much emphasis on loving each other? Because it is the key to the kingdom. It is a time-tested learning experience. God commands us to love even our enemies, and if we don't practice love on our neighbors, it is ludicrous to think we will ever love the lost men of this world.

The Lord has shown me that we foster innate affections for those closest to us. But being hurt and disappointed by one person will sometimes diminish the scope of our concern for another. Yet godly, unconditional love is quite different. Not a natural inclination from the heart, true love is both supernatural and costly. The love of God requires a long-term commitment and the keeping of short accounts whenever you feel betrayed.

There are two things that make this revelation so important: First, the world will know that this kind of love is divine evidence that God is alive in us. Second, we can only pull it off when Jesus is seated upon the throne of our hearts. This in turn releases all of His power into our lives, thus enabling us to overcome any obstacle before us.

As I read about people like William Booth, founder of the Salvation Army; Millard Fuller, founder of Habitat for Humanity; evangelist John Staggers; and the countless others who dedicate everything they have, sacrificing time and resources in doing whatever they can to improve the chances for so many lost and lonely souls, I know it's Him. I see God at work through their love. His presence in our lives makes us change the way we love. Suddenly we start to give people in need of a break the benefit of the doubt. It makes us remember that everybody's got a story.

Take off your disguise, drop your guard for a moment, and tell me yours. If you made it in this world, you didn't pull yourself up by your own bootstraps. You had help from someone. Perhaps it's time you share your success with another person. You won't have to go far to find someone who needs your help.

22
A Time to Lead

The statistics are staggering: 25,000 men opted to throw in the towel and commit suicide this past year. Did anyone close to them know that life for these men was so discouraging that death seemed the better choice? Tens of thousands of teenage girls became pregnant. Even more decided to take the lives of their unborn children through the national tragedy of abortion. It is estimated that 60,000 homeless people will sleep on the streets of America tonight, unloved and unprotected. And, like Rachel mourning for her children in Ramah, the mothers of babies in Bosnia, Russia, Mozambique, Sudan, Ethiopia, North Korea, Romania, India, Pakistan, Iraq, Haiti, Ireland, Palestine, South America, China, and our own inner cities of America weep for the future of their families.

Clearly, an erosion of rock-solid confidence in tomorrow is taking place, leaving behind a marshland of hopelessness and despair for many. Can you see the hungering hearts of our children, sorely in need of a hero? Do you notice the hollow stares of our nation's outcasts, who have no one to speak for them? A rising tide may lift all boats, but it does little for the people left standing on the shore. Instead of the high-sounding slogans and pat answers for complex arguments, by now we must realize it is time to lead.

Leading in the World

I believe God is sick and tired of listening to intelligent men and women disagree so energetically about the reasons for "the least that are among us," then shifting into boring rhetoric during discussions to find solutions. We seem content to blame the suffering of many of our people—the empty-bellied babies, holders of second-class citizenship, and those without access to power—on everything except the will to do what is necessary to solve the problem. Is the only message we have for our most vulnerable citizens as they go to bed each night one that says they are to blame?

As tiresome as listening to a roll call of statistics can be at times, it is clear God is saying to His people, "Wake up! Be my hands and feet! Serve those in need!" When the world can see the family of God in all of its diversity cooperating together to help others, radically loving one another as God in Christ loves us, it will distract them from their idols and challenge them to accept God's invitation to come and be saved.

Why is this so hard to understand? Because we are still afraid of what love will cost us. It will cost you everything. Consider for a moment what love cost God: the life of His only begotten Son. *If the amount God paid for loving the world came with such a high price tag, we must also arm ourselves with the mind-set that love is not cheap.* When it costs you something of value, when it pleases you to give it away to someone for their good, without conditions and with no hidden agenda, it is love. God wants men to begin leading in the world by demonstrating that kind of love to those in need.

Looking back over my life, I reminded God how much I was already contributing toward the betterment of mankind. But the Lord warned me not to be deceived because I go to church and pay my tithes. It is a good thing to volunteer as a part of the neighborhood watch; however, we should not allow ourselves to be lulled to sleep because of our good works. We cannot be satisfied because we coach Little League baseball on the weekend, or attend church meetings regularly, or drop a monthly check in the offering plate. Tom Skinner once told me, "God desires to live His life through you with no help from you." So if I am impressed with how much I am doing for God, I have been duped by the devil. *Doing more* is not God's goal for my life. Being more like Him is the goal.

I once read that God is not looking for a leader; He's looking for a man He can lead. Could that man be you? Practice, starting with those closest to you. Stand in front of the mirror in your prayer closet and say, "It is time for this man to lead in love."

Loving Your Wife

A second area in which we must lead is marriage. We are called to lead by loving our wives—setting an example that is as pure and holy as the relationship Christ has with His church. If I love my wife as much as Christ loves the church, I'll be willing to do what is necessary to build up her emotional and physical security, putting her needs ahead of my own in order to please her.

The picture of this single truth was made perfectly clear to me recently, after Bunny and I had completed a powerful week of ministry in Bermuda, teaching from our book *The Master's Degree: Majoring in Your Marriage.* At the conference, we had witnessed the healing of relationships, the strengthening of families, the saving of souls, the reclaiming of backsliders, and the redirection of single men and women's lives. Homes were restored and marriages healed, and I was feeling pretty good about myself. That all came to an end in one night.

Approaching our last two days on the island by playing tennis and worshiping the Lord together, Bunny and I found a wonderfully picturesque restaurant where we wanted to go for their lamb dinner. But on Monday morning, the day before our departure, I was invited to try my hand at a little fishing. I was thrilled! After all, fishing is one of my favorite pastimes for relaxation. It never dawned on me that this was not the perfect way to end our week in Bermuda. When my driver picked me up from the pier to rendezvous with Bunny back at the hotel, it was nearly mealtime.

As I told her about my plans for a fish fry, I realized there was some sort of problem. She reminded me that I had promised to go out to dinner at that posh restaurant located on the bay. Not to worry, I thought, we will just call ahead, place an order for the lamb, pick it up, and take it back to the hotel and eat it in our room. Then later we would dine sumptuously on the fish I had caught.

On the way to the restaurant, Bunny's jaws were so tight she couldn't talk. *How am I going to fix this?* I wondered. In my view, since I was going to pick up the meal for her, we would still both have what we wanted for dinner. But clearly I was missing the point.

Hoping to expel some of the chill in the air, I made the suggestion we stay and eat dinner at the restaurant. Nothing worked. Bunny was not going to settle for a rushed meal. Nothing I could say was going to help out the evening's debacle—except, perhaps, an apology and a complete change of plans. I didn't consider that an option. We brought the meal back to the hotel, she picked at it, and later I had my fish fry at the pastor's house.

The next day, seated in the lounge of the airport terminal on our way back to the States, the minor squall turned into a major storm. What began as a mature discussion of differences turned into harsh words and silly accusations. When the smoke finally cleared, there were two emotionally exhausted, severely wounded people stretched out in the chairs at the gate. We traveled back to Los Angeles with Bunny seated on the opposite side of the airplane, which was fine with me. Once home, the cool breeze turned into a cold freeze. Eventually she suggested we talk with an outsider to settle our differences—something I jumped at, "knowing" I was right.

While waiting, I began to see how the devil had taken advantage of our tiredness from that week, catching us completely off guard and smoothly orchestrating this entire fiasco.

In retrospect, I was wrong about how I handled things. Here I was in one of the most romantic spots of the world, bordered by the bluest of ocean waters and a naturally green, plushly manicured landscape in a remote location, and I chose to go to an evening fish fry. An ideal day for nurturing love, and I badly mangled it.

I must admit, though, that I had help. I had my own private analyst talking into my ears day and night, assuring me of how right I was. One morning the Spirit of the Lord interrupted our discussion and asked me point-blank, "How much of a price are you willing to pay for being right, mighty man of God?" Once again, He reminded me that, "*Being* right is not as important as *doing* right."

The Lord forced me to reevaluate my response to the situation and decide whether or not the price for making me feel better was worth the cost of a hurt relationship with my wife. Pride, He showed me again, is like a drug in the life of the addict. It dulls your senses, gives you a false sense of security, and it never knows when to say that's enough. One thing I knew for sure, more than anything else and anyone on earth, I loved none like Bunny. So then, what was I going to do about it? Suddenly, that became my priority and the focus of my energy.

Once God cured my mental constipation and got me back to thinking right, He gave me a plan, consisting of an apology, love notes, flowers, and a steady parade of stimulating surprises. "Kill her with kindness," He said, "overwhelm her with affection, and plead temporary insanity."

How many times have I taught other men, "Husbands, likewise, dwell with them with understanding, giving honor to the wife, as to the weaker vessel, and as being heirs together of the grace of life, that your prayers may not be hindered" (1 Peter 3:7). I was dwelling with Bunny as my servant, not as a fellow heir. I failed to lead with love, and it was my responsibility to make it right.

If you are married, more than likely you, too, have read this convicting verse of Scripture. And perhaps like me, you failed to work it into your routine on a daily basis. Jesus says, "If you know these things . . ."—meaning instruction from His Word intended for success in life—"happy are ye." You're in bad shape if you do not know His Word, but even if you do, when you are not applying it, you're no better off.

Well, take for instance His instructions about your wife. It is better, God's Word says, for a man to dwell upon the roof of his house or someplace out in the desert, than for him to live in a house with a contentious wife. Now, God is not trying to get the man to move out into a desert. He is simply saying that if you fail to get an understanding about her, and neglect to do what you know you should, you're not going to be a happy man.

"If you know these things, blessed are you if you do them" (John 13:17).

God showed me that all I had to do to solve that situation was to love my wife the way that He loves me.

Lead in Loving Children

The third area a man must learn to lead is the family. I have heard it said again and again that the greatest gift a father can give his children is for them to see him loving their mother. Certainly if this were played out in the sanctuary of marriages, divorce would suffer a major setback.

Divorce is a cruel hoax to prey upon the minds of unsuspecting children. They will always wonder if they have done enough to contribute toward stabilizing the home and saving the marriage. At their young and impressionable ages, children don't realize that it's the parents, not the child, who are responsible for keeping the marriage intact. Divorce is often the offspring of selfishness. Tragically, the children of divorce will usually suffer from low self-esteem later in life, and the parents will be too selfish to see it.

Many times the spirit of divorce invades a household long before a physical separation takes place. If and when counsel is sought, often the couple has already decided to throw in the towel. They think they've waited too long to rediscover the smoldering spark of romance and the will to try it again. But that is not true. My conclusion is that birthing a successful marriage comes as the result of sacrifice and hard labor. But someone must take the reins of leadership. If you will sweat it out, the dividends are worth the investment.

If you have children, they deserve your marriage at its best, for they are a heritage from the Lord. Of our six children, each one of them has a special place in our hearts. Our commitment remains, even when they make mistakes. I love them, even when I've felt hurt by them. I'm trying to be like my heavenly Father. When my actions have led to near disaster, He stands steady and assures me, saying, "Frank, no matter what you are going through right now, it is not your destiny. 'For I know the thoughts that I think toward you . . . thoughts of peace and not of evil, to give you a future and a hope' (Jeremiah 29:11)."

Therefore, the more I mature as a father, the more I realize that an earthly father's love for his children ought to be unconditional as well. How we act toward them should be predicated upon two things: preparing them to meet God, and guiding them toward a secure future.

Begin to practice the following. Dedicate your children to the Lord. Educate them about the Lord. Stimulate them to desire to know the Lord for themselves. When I pray each morning for our children, I ask God for four favors:

1. Save my kids,

2. Sanctify their hearts,

3. Keep them safe, and

4. Help them to succeed.

Every Monday, Bunny and I fast and pray specifically for each of our children. And though in the past we have seen them make costly errors in the pursuit of personal priorities, pleasure, and prestige, through answered prayer we have witnessed miraculous turnabouts in the focuses of their lives. We are seeing daily evidence of their salvation, acknowledgments of their sanctification, an experiencing of God's protection over them, and progressive signs of their impending success in life.

We fathers must continue to take the time to love our children. If your children are constantly straddling the fence, finding themselves in harm's way, or walking down the road of rebelliousness, I challenge you to fast one day a week (from sunup to sundown), and pray for your children by name. You will be richly blessed. Give God time to reach them at their level, and wait for the miracle to reveal itself. Above all, lead them in love, setting an example of godliness for them to follow. Don't just point to them the way, show them. And if they stray, never give up, father. Remember what the Bible says: "There is hope in your future, says the LORD, that your children shall come back to their own border" (Jeremiah 31:17).

23
Personal Test, Private Matter

One of the benefits of developing relationships with other men is that they can surround you when you face trials and tribulations. Let me tell you about one of the many times my own spirituality was severely tested. Since my daughter Fawn was ten, all she had ever wanted to be was grown-up. We were having tremendous problems disciplining her when she was a teenager, and I was at the end of my rope. Fawn went to church with us every Sunday, but still challenged me as to the soundness of my faith in the existence of God, the origin of the Bible, and the ritual of church.

I was beginning to feel the devil had successfully planted an enemy agent inside my own house, infiltrating it through the womb of my wife. Fawn was so negative that if she smiled, you should worry. But in reality, she hardly ever smiled. From an early age, seldom did any of our family pictures (snapped with or without her awareness and permission) portray a portrait of happiness. She became increasingly disrespectful of Bunny and me and the rod of correction was doing no good. It seemed as if there was nothing anyone could do to change her.

Finally, when she was 16 years of age, Fawn left our home. For our own legal protection, Bunny and I decided to emancipate her. She moved in with a girlfriend of hers in a government housing project. My faith was never tested as much as it was during this period of my life. No other family, marital, or financial pressures were ever as great as the one we felt regarding Fawn. We prayed mightily and often for her.

I am grateful to God that I had brothers I could call and to whom I could tell the truth. In them I had close friends—guys I could share my thoughts with, revealing what I was going through emotionally, without feeling like a failure as a father. From my brothers in the faith I drew strength and encouragement to hold on and trust the Lord.

Private Test

For several weeks I didn't talk to Fawn at all. Then one day, the young girl whose family she was living with called and asked, "Mr. Wilson, what does Fawn have to do to come back home?" I told her, "Fawn already knows she can come home anytime. But she also knows what she has to do before she comes—apologize for what she's done and be respectful to her parents."

We didn't hear from Fawn again for weeks, except on those infrequent occasions when she would phone to say hi and tell us "everything's fine." Three weeks later, she moved in with another girlfriend of hers, this time in an equally rough area of Los Angeles. Whenever we heard from her, Fawn always made it sound as though everything was fine. However, one time I sensed some fear and apprehension in her voice. She told me that the girl she was staying with had a boyfriend who had been making angry threats. It was apparent she was concerned for their safety. She also needed some of her clothes from the house and wondered if I would mind bringing them to her. I agreed. After I arrived, Fawn and her girlfriend decided to come back with me to our home and visit for a while.

I prayed and prayed, but I never invited our daughter to move back home. I wanted to, but I felt I had to trust the Lord to work things out in Fawn's life. The more we talked, the more I sensed movement in her life. Eventually she moved into a group home for runaway teenage girls. When she wanted to come and visit us or go job-hunting, she would call, and I would travel to pick her up. The supervisors always liked her, and would tell me privately Fawn didn't belong in those types of facilities. They would often give her some type of responsibility for running a part of the program, or assign her some administrative duties for a few hours each day.

It was during that time someone asked me, "Since you have emancipated her and placed her on her own, why are you helping her?" My answer was simple: Fawn was my daughter. The things I was doing for her were things I would want someone to do for me.

Finally, Fawn started visiting more frequently and bringing an outfit or two of her clothing. Each time she would leave a little more behind at our house. One day as she was walking through the kitchen, she showed Bunny her business card, and it had our address on it! Bunny asked her, "Fawn, are you trying to move back home?" With that, Fawn apologized and we allowed her to return home.

A Public Victory

It was clear to us that God had done a marvelous work in our daughter's life. She was a different person. Her spirit was calmer, her countenance softer. After a few months, she began to baby-sit for her older sister's children, eventually moving in with her and her family. Like a butterfly, Fawn slowly blossomed. Her personality is precious, her smile arresting, and her spirit splendid.

One of the nicest changes was that she began asking a million and one questions about the Bible. Today our daughter is totally dedicated to Christ and is a great influence on the rest of her sisters. In fact, each of our children has proven influential in the lives of the others.

The miracle of it is that the whole time Fawn was on her own as a kid in a grown-up world, God kept her safe, protecting her from harm. There must have been thousands of angels around her, for she lived near some dangerous places. She never was interested in drugs or cigarettes, and seemed to have minimal interest in boys at the time. As a rebellious young person, Fawn simply thought she wanted to be out and on her own. Bunny and I prayed fervently through the entire ordeal, always looking to the Lord for guidance and comfort.

Through it all, I learned to appreciate the power of unity between a man and his wife, and the value of the support of brothers. My friends identified with my emotional insecurity when my faith was put to the test.

Leading and Loving

As a husband and father, I am charged with loving and leading my family. Some people are almost impossible to love, yet God commands me to love them anyway. Persons I allow to get close to me are sometimes the most difficult. Yet Jesus said to His disciples after washing their feet, "If I then, your Lord and Teacher, have washed your feet, you also ought to wash one another's feet. For I have given you an example, that you should do as I have done to you" (John 13:14,15). Christ, our Leader, wants us to follow His example—leading and loving those around us.

Consider for a moment how much God loves us. He came to where we were in order to reach out to us. We don't have to find a hidden God—nor clean ourselves up to become acceptable to Him. Not only that, He has compassion on our condition. He knows how we feel. God came as a simple man, offering help and healing to those in need. In the same way, if I am to follow His example, I will need to offer myself as best I can in ways that reach out to others.

God looked beyond my faults and saw my need. I must train myself to follow that example of love and look for the potential in each person, not just his or her failings and flaws. God is committed to my growth. He doesn't focus on my weaknesses, but on the development of my strengths for His purposes. He sees a future for me and is most concerned with my complete recovery, not just my current relief. As a leader, I must maintain a constant interest in helping other people succeed, while recognizing that the best thing I can do for anyone is tell them about the Lord Jesus. To love is to know for certain God is alive on the inside of you. His resurrection power, in all its magnificence and splendor, is enthroned in your heart. He is with you in the personal tests, the private matters, and all of your future endeavors.

24
The Road to Maturity

Someone once asked me, "How do you learn how to love someone?"

My answer was simple: "How do you learn anything? You *practice.* Love is the same way. We learn how to love as we practice loving."

No matter how spiritual we say we are, love takes practice.

A few months ago, I got together with some of the brothers for a time of sharing and prayer. It was an extraordinary session of transparency and power. Starting with individual periods of worship and petitions, we prayed for about two hours, climaxing in a symphony of praises. The power of the Lord was evident to all of those present. During the period we call "afterglow," Joseph Garlington called to our attention a poignant portrait of spiritual unity.

"Did you notice the entire time as we were praying, even though we are of different denominations, there was a dynamic flow of God's anointing and the peace of His presence?" Every man in that room was in love with Jesus, and was literally having fun just being with Him and with one another. This wasn't hard work; it was joyful celebration!

The power was in the connection we all felt with each other and the Lord, not in the words or the work of our prayers. If you're not connecting with Him and with each other when you pray, you're nothing but "sounding brass and tinkling cymbals."

The ability to communicate with the Almighty, the omniscient and omnipresent One, is a gift and a privilege. When we understand that, we protect it. Broken relationships with one another can cause our fellowship with God to be broken. Not only do I want a free flow of information from me to God, I want that same open channel coming from God to me. Besides, the Lord works through the men He has placed with me when we pray together.

Made in the Image of God

A man is the image and the glory of God; therefore, according to 1 Corinthians 16:13, we are commanded to "Act like men!" In other words, *"Grow up!"* The Apostle Paul is saying to you, "Be a man." That means taking a mature man's view of God, recognizing His sovereignty over us, and trusting in His leadership. It also means taking a man's view of other men, trusting in them and working together with them for God's holy purposes.

Jesus taught that "if you bring your gift to the altar, and there remember that your brother has something against you, leave your gift there before the altar, and go your way. First, be reconciled [apologize] to your brother, and then come and offer your gift" (Matthew 5:23,24). There are times when, as we're praying, it becomes evident there is a problem between two men. That is the time to stop and resolve it, before it becomes a hidden spiritual problem.

If we're going to be mature men in the Lord, it means we stop attacking others in order to make ourselves feel better. It means we need to stop blaming others for our lack of success. It means we need to cease from accusing our wives of causing our marital troubles. "If any of you lacks wisdom, let him ask of God," James 1:5 says. Success in anything comes from the Lord. If I am not being promoted at work, I had better go to God and find out why, because promotions come from God. It is childish of me to blame others for my mistakes or failures, and to not take responsibility for my marriage. God put the man in charge of the family, and if we ruin it with our selfishness or lack of understanding, we cannot blame our wives. It is childish of me to be wrong and not be man enough to admit it—childish to be lost and pretend not to be.

When Paul was writing to the church at Corinth, he told them, "When I was a child, I spoke as a child, I understood as a child, I thought as a child; but when I became a man, I put away childish things" (1 Corinthians 13:11). When I got married, my wife deserved a man. When I became a father, my children deserved a man. Positionally, I am already the image and the glory of God right now, according to Scripture. I'm a man to them and a man of God and my masculinity should be a reflection of that. But experientially, manhood is mine to attain. It requires my acting like a man, setting an example of righteousness and diligence in my home. Becoming a man will mean thinking of other's needs ahead of my own, since they are under my care.

Do you know what Christ's brother James said about maturing as a man?

> Be doers of the word, and not hearers only, deceiving yourselves. For if anyone is a hearer of the word and not a doer, he is like a man observing his natural face in a mirror; for he

observes himself, goes away, and immediately
forgets what kind of man he was. But he who
looks into the perfect law of liberty and continues
in it, and is not a forgetful hearer but a doer of the
work, this one will be blessed in what he does
(James 1:22-25).

A man doesn't just know what to do—he does it. A
man does the right thing, even when it's difficult. And a
man is blessed by God for his faithfulness and obedience.

Looking in the Mirror

Men, the first thing we must do is take off our masks.
Then we can look into the mirror and see what God's man
is like. Next we break out our Bibles and see what God's
Word calls us to be. Compare the man in the mirror to the
man in Scripture. If I look into the Bible and see myself as
a husband, I had better be following His plan for hus-
banding. *Husband* comes from the root words *House band.*
It is his responsibility to hold the house together. When I
see what I'm to do and put it into practice, the Lord
rewards me with blessing. But if I don't, it's like looking
in the mirror, seeing that I need a shave, then turning
away and forgetting all about it. Only a fool does that.
However, before I can see myself, I've got to take off my
mask, be honest about myself, and gaze into the mirror of
God's holy Word.

One Thursday morning while waiting for the meeting
to start, I was seated next to a dear friend who had only
started coming to the men's fellowship about two weeks
before. He said to me, "Frank, you wouldn't believe what
happened to me yesterday. My wife packed up everything. She packed up the kids, packed up the furniture,
and while I was at work she just moved out. I don't know
where she went."

Trying to be as comforting as possible, I asked him, "What was going on? Were you guys having problems?"

He just looked at me and said, "No, man. We weren't having any problems."

That's when I knew something was wrong. A wife doesn't just move out without a reason. This man had a far bigger challenge than his wife leaving him. In my view, the brother was visually impaired. He couldn't see things right in his face. He would go to church on Sunday mornings, look into the mirror of God's Word, recognize it didn't reflect his own life, then immediately forget what it said as soon as he went home. He was a fool and needed to put the Lord's principles into practice.

A wife will tell you again and again when there are problems in the relationship. Next, she will start to show you. If you fail to see all of those signs, your wife may assume that her leaving will not be missed either. Your vision impairment may have caused you to miss the first signs, but there's no way you can miss the sign of her packing up and moving out!

I began talking with that man about being a godly husband, and we put a plan together for getting his family back. The hardest part was not creating the plan, but helping him look into the mirror and understand that the responsibility was his. Once he did that, he won back his wife.

Of Fathers and Forgiveness

Like any man, I carry a bit of baggage from my father. I think we're all shaped by our dads in some ways. One time, while I was attending a conference at the Mount Hermon conference center, I spoke to a young man about his relationship with his father. He was very bitter because his dad wasn't there for him, had never done anything for him, or helped prepare him in any way. Now this young man was a father, and though he desired to be a good dad, he realized his ability to father had been shaped by his own absentee dad.

I told him, "Son, your dad may not have been the best, but whatever it was that your dad had to give, he gave it to you. Maybe your grandfather never threw his arms around your dad and said, 'Son, I love you.' If no one ever said it to him, how could he say it to you? Unless he was challenged by someone he could look up to, what model did he have to follow? Everything you and I need to know about being a father and a man is mapped out in the Word of God. Take what your dad made you and wash it in the Word. Then obey the Scriptures. Be the father God is calling you to be."

In the movie *Dad*, a young man grows up estranged from his father, a man for whom he has little respect. The son always believed that Mom ran the show and walked all over his dad. When he became an adult, the son left home for the world of business, hitting it big in New York as a corporate executive. He had not been back home for years when he received the news that his mom was seriously ill. Taking a few days to go and see about her, he arrives in town and moves into the house with his dad.

The two men began spending a lot of time together, knocking around the house and talking about their lives growing up together. Soon the son discovered, to his amazement, that his father was not such a bad guy after all.

When I watched that movie, I thought about some of my brothers and the rocky relationships they have with their fathers. It's interesting how easy it is to judge another person based on a fraction of the facts. Most of us, as boys, had no idea of the pressures our dads were under just to survive and feed our families. And then there are men who have simply abandoned their wife and kids. I cannot pretend to understand their story. They have one, I'm certain.

Everybody does. In the movie, after a few weeks of warm and wonderful conversation, they started to bond. The son began to see life on a more mature level because he better understood what his dad had been through.

It sometimes seems as though God, whose ways are past finding out, allows bad things to happen in one instance so that good things will occur in another. For example, when Lazarus became ill, Jesus could have prevented his friend's death. He chose not to. Why? So that the glory of God might be revealed in the raising of Lazarus from the dead. Jesus wanted to display His power in order to teach His followers about His power over life and death. Nothing could have affirmed the divinity of Jesus Christ more than raising a man who had been dead three days. He allowed something bad to happen so that something greater could occur.

That same process happens in our own lives. Sometimes the Lord allows trouble to come upon us in order to help us grow, or to teach us, or to help shape our character. Your father might not have set a godly example, but God didn't make him your father by mistake. The Lord wanted you as that man's son, and if you can forgive his failings, you can grow according to God's plan into fatherhood.

Showing Up for Work

The son in the movie had also become estranged from his own young son due to his workaholic habits. Getting back with his dad helped him become a better parent as well.

Being a father is hard work. It means thinking about other people, keeping track of their needs, and sometimes helping with things you don't really understand. A father I know, raised in a family of boys, now has three daughters. He has no idea why they say the things they do, or why they burst out crying for no apparent reason, and he admits most of the time he is stumped when asked questions about fashion, emotion, and toys. But he figures the Lord gave him those girls, so it's his responsibility to show up and help however he can. He's faithful to the Lord in every way possible—even though he often doesn't feel like he knows what he's doing.

Sometimes we can't win in life, so we trust in the Lord and rely on His grace. We humbly obey Him, riding through the rough spots and knowing He is in control. Parenting can be a humbling experience, because it reminds us that we're not always in control. But if you're a father, the least you can do is show up and set an example of love and faithfulness.

In the movie I mentioned earlier, the mother improves while the father gets sick with cancer. The son visits the hospital every day, spending time sharing life experiences. Just before dying, the father tells his son, "As I was sleeping last night, I was thinking about the year of 1947, and one of the greatest moments in history." He talks of baseball—a World Series game between the Brooklyn Dodgers and the New York Yankees. In the dugout sat a young kid, a guy who had been at the end of the bench all year, looking toward the manager and hoping for a chance to play. The manager never called his name. But on this particular day, the regular right fielder for Brooklyn was injured and the manager decided to take a chance on the youngster. "Hey, son," he barked, "grab your glove and go into right field."

"Yes, sir!" the nervous kid replied, barely pausing long enough to grab his cap. The score was tied 2 to 2, with two men on base in the ninth inning, and star center fielder Joe DiMaggio at the plate. DiMaggio took the first strike, swung and missed at the second, then stroked a long hit directly to right field. The ball started heading toward the right-field fence. Everybody in the park knew it was a home run. DiMaggio knew it was a home run. But somebody forgot to tell the kid filling in at right field. The young man got up all of his speed, leaped high in the air, and just as the ball was about to leave the park, he stretched out as far as he could and snagged it for the third out. The crowd went wild! DiMaggio kicked the dirt in disgust.

At that point, the father stopped telling his story and looked at his son. "Do you know what that means?" After a pause he said, "Anything is possible, as long as you just show up for work." Sometimes being a great parent isn't found in doing anything flashy, or having the most money, or being the biggest success. It's found in spending time, showing love, and being patient with our kids. "I wish," he continued, "I had hugged you more . . . told you I loved you more."

Don't we all wish our fathers had just shown up more? If so, then we can learn from that lesson by showing up ourselves. It's not too late, regardless how old your children are. As a father and as a husband, I plan to show up. As a son, a brother, and a friend, I plan to show up. Life will always provide me an opportunity. God will give me the strength. I've made mistakes, and the Lord knows I'll probably make more of them, but by His grace I will do my best to reveal His love to my family.

Brother, there is still time. Call your parents, put your kids on your calendar, or take your wife for a walk. Upgrade your insurance policy or plan your estate, no matter the size of it, to take care of your family even after you're gone. Take the time now to show your family how much you love them.

25
The Myth About Bootstraps

My father did not attend even one sporting event in which I was a participant. As far as I can remember, he never came to any of my meets or games, and I went out for every sport known to mankind, searching for significance in my life. I don't recall my dad even even showing up for my graduation from high school. So for me, success in life at anything was a priority. I suppose I wanted to impress my father.

In all fairness, both my mom and dad worked hard day and night. But try using that as an excuse on a 13-year-old who has no idea what life is all about. I usually did well in school, but I knew I needed something extra if I was going to get out of the rut of my neighborhood. Following in the footsteps of most of the men I knew in our community, including my father's, left me with few options for aspiring to a better life. Dad had a job as a laborer for the Firestone Tire Company. It was a good, honest living, but the wages were low. He sacrificed and did all he could to take care of his children, but I knew he could not afford to send me to college. Still, I wanted something better for my life. Most of all, I wanted him to see in me my potential. Perhaps if just one time he had shown up for something I did, or put his big, strong hands around me and said I was going to be something great in life, I might have felt he was there for me, that he believed in me. He never did.

Search for Success

By the time I reached the eleventh grade, I had struck out in every sport I had attempted, badly torn the cartilage in my right knee, and was peering straight into the face of a fouled-up future. Hobbling across the football practice field after school one day, on the way from another treatment for my banged-up knee, a friend on the track team asked me, "Frank, have you ever considered pole-vaulting?" Of course I hadn't—track had never even come up for discussion. I didn't really know what the pole vault was, except that it looked dangerous. You ran down a track, were vaulted way up in the air, then had to land in a small pit of sawdust to keep from getting slammed on the pavement. However, the coach told me the only pole-vaulter on the team was a senior, and there would be no one to take his place.

The more I thought about it, the better it sounded. I had exhausted every other avenue to reach my goal of going to college on an athletic scholarship and having a better economic future than my parents. And while I never failed to make the honor roll, the option of a scholarship for my academic achievements was never brought up by anyone. So the idea of pole-vaulting began to sound like an excellent suggestion. In my junior year of high school, I was horrible. I couldn't even clear the minimum height requirements. But in the city championship meet my senior year, I vaulted nine feet six inches. I know that athletes can almost high jump that height today, but everybody has to start somewhere, and that accomplishment qualified me for the state meet. I came in third place. That third-place finish in turn qualified me for participation in the southwest conference championship meet. It felt like that meet lasted the entire night. I jumped and jumped until, with only one other person left in the competition, the bar was raised to a height that would establish a new conference record. My opponent filed out. I was the only vaulter remaining in the competition.

Looking back, it was unthinkable that I could not only win such an important meet, but set a new record while doing so. I remember racing down the runway, pole held high above my head, perspiration pouring down my forehead. As I planted the pole, I felt as though a wind came up under me, picked me up, and threw me over that bar. Falling into the cushioned pit, I was ecstatic!

Because of that jump I received numerous four-year scholarship offers from schools throughout the region. Through that turn of events and others, I made my way up the ladder to success, always believing I was doing it myself. Looking at all of the plaques and awards on my wall, I thought I "pulled myself up by my own bootstraps."

It was many years later before I realized it was the good philosophies drilled into my head as a kid, and the prayers of loved ones who had aided my success by asking the heavenly Father to help me. Many times God came along beside to carry and hoist me over difficult barriers that blocked my life, and I failed to acknowledge Him. I had to learn *how to recognize the hand of God in my personal history.* As I reflected on my past, I began to see God's hand upon my life. How did I make it past that roadblock? How did I escape a dead-end street? Who saved me from the consequences of that near-fatal disaster? It wasn't my own doing, but the hand of the Lord.

Pushed Up

God is at work in our lives. He watches over all things. If you will take a moment and think about it, you can see His hand in all the turning points of your life. We don't pull ourselves up—He pushes us up whenever we reach our limitations.

Get rid of the baggage that boasts, "I did it my way," and begin looking to Him for guidance. Your way has left behind a long string of broken relationships, a list of things done that you wish you could change. Success is not a destiny; it's a journey. And as it has already been shown, in order to succeed at anything you will need lots of help along the way. If God withdrew His breath from you for a mere ten minutes, you would be brain-dead. Think about a time you were discouraged. Perhaps a perfect stranger brightened up your day with a word, and he did not even know what you were going through. God selects people like Joshua and Caleb to assist those like Moses and Aaron. He enlists persons on the order of Barnabas, Mark, and Silas to walk with and support others like Peter and Paul. Ezra, whose name means "God helps," was sent by God from Babylon to remind the children of Israel about the one whose name is Jehovah. He has used special people to help you in your life as well. It is because He is our "Ezra," our Helper.

God wants to do more in our lives, if we will let Him. He desires to take us to that next level of supernatural existence. And He can, but we must learn to trust Him. Start by listening to the witness of the Scriptures, reading the Bible daily. You see, once you recognize the history of His participation in your life, it's important that you offer Him the opportunity to influence your thoughts. Pick up your Bible each morning and spend some time reading His Word. Through it, you will learn that God has a specific plan and purpose for your life. You will learn to hear His voice as He speaks to you.

Study His Word carefully so that you will not wander away from Him in pursuit of your own will or what someone else tells you. If you want to build your trust in God, recognize His hand, know His Word, and begin to stretch your faith every day.

In order for me to strengthen my discipline, it is important that I exercise regularly. One of the exercises I do is sit-ups. A few years ago I noticed my stomach was beginning to take on the appearance of a melon. Throughout most of my life it had been flat, but suddenly I started to look like I was pregnant. I began an exercise program to help fix the problem—ten sit-ups the first day, adding one more each day. When I reached 120 sit-ups, I decided to stay there and incorporate some additional techniques into my workout program.

The road from 10 sit-ups to 120 was never easy. Even after I had been doing them for a while, some mornings a little voice would come into my head and ask, "Why are you putting your body through all of this torture?" Some mornings I would listen, but almost always I would tell the voice to shut up. I knew why I was doing it—for the discipline I needed and the rewards I would receive.

In the same way, faith to obey God must be exercised. For instance, the Bible says, "Be kindly affectionate to one another with brotherly love in honor giving preference to one another" (Romans 12:10). Once you've mastered that principle, a few verses later we read, "Therefore 'If your enemy is hungry, feed him; if he is thirsty give him a drink' " (verse 20). It takes faith to pull this off.

Remember, *target practice does not determine how good you will be in battle, just how well you aim.*

The image of the Lord's glory is mirrored by His Word. As you and I study and submit to it, we are changed into that same image, from glory to glory. If our desire is to be like the Lord, by faith we have to take our masks off.

Take another brother or two along on your journey and discover together who is "the man behind the mask."

We All Need a Brother

The other day, I was sitting in the lobby of a hotel in Universal City, reviewing some notes prior to entering a board meeting. From across the room I heard a loud voice call out my name.

"Frank! Frank Wilson!"

I raised my head to see who it was, and there stood Reggie Williams, outside linebacker for the Cincinnati Bengals. I had not seen Reggie for more than nine years. The last time I spoke with him, he was running for public office in a city on the East Coast. Many of the other brothers had stayed in close contact with him.

"How have you been?" he asked. "How's Bunny and the family?"

"Fine," I responded, "and yours?"

"Oh, everybody's great. I'm living in Orlando now. I'm one of the directors for Disney." Reggie was in town for the dedication of an educational training facility built for the youth in Los Angeles, donated by the NFL foundation.

"Frank," he said to me, "if you're ever traveling toward Orlando, let me know you're coming and I will roll out the red carpet for you."

After a few minutes of hugging and sharing how really good it was to see each other again, I turned and started to head up the hallway for my meeting.

"By the way, Frank," he called after me, "I need a brother to walk with me." Then he smiled and went on his way.

I thought to myself as I waved back to him, "Yeah, and don't we all?"

Other Good
Harvest House Reading

The Master's Degree
Frank and Bunny Wilson

This book explores the spiritual, emotional, and physical aspects of marriage, then shows how God views, supports, and participates in every marriage.

A Father for All Seasons
Bob Welch

Using plenty of amusing anecdotes and great sports stories, this book offers encouragement to dads and sons by reiterating an important message: Fathers need sons, sons need fathers, and the world is a better place when the two connect.

A Look at Life from a Deer Stand
Steve Chapman

Taking you to the heart of deer country, Steve Chapman shares his humorous and exciting experiences and his discovery of the amazing parallels between what happens during the hunt and what takes place in our walks with God.

In a Mirror Dimly
Roger Corey

An American doctor seeking escape from the pain of a tragic accident finds himself working in a refugee camp on a remote island as he struggles to find a reason to go on living. His life takes a dramatic turn when a young Vietnamese woman arrives at his clinic with a life-threatening injury, and an unknown enemy disrupts his newfound happiness and threatens the safety of the camp.